COVID-19, Education, and Literacy in Malaysia

Part of a mini series of Focus books on COVID-19 in Malaysia, the chapters in this book address the pandemic's impacts on education and literacy.

Covering a range of teaching and learning challenges impacting learners and teachers, the contributors highlight the pervasiveness of the pandemic on Malaysian society and how Malaysians have found ways to cope. They focus mainly on students' COVID-19 narratives, digital and health literacy issues, language, and new vocabulary. This is an opportunity to witness how researchers from multiple disciplines can join forces during challenging times. There are a great many lessons to be learned from the successes and failures in responding to the pandemic and the measures that have been necessary to contain it.

A fascinating read for scholars and educators with an interest in crisis management in non-Western contexts, especially those with a particular interest in Malaysia, or Southeast Asia more generally.

Ambigapathy Pandian (The chief editor of literacy and education book) is the Dean, Faculty of Language and Communication, University Malaysia Sarawak (UNIMAS). As a scholar, Professor Ambigapathy Pandian's field of research interests include, language, literacy education, and Teaching English to Speakers of Other Languages. Ambigapathy has delivered webinars related to COVID-19, such as "Research in the Arts, Humanities and Management: Normal, New Normal, Abnormal?". He is the author and editor of more than 60 books published with Scholar's Press, Cambridge Scholar Publishing, Oxford Fajar Press, Lang Publishers (New York) and Common Ground Publications (Australia), and many articles featured in prestigious international journals.

Surinderpal Kaur (The editor of *COVID-19 in Malaysia* multidisciplinary series) is an Associate Professor and Dean at the Faculty of

Languages and Linguistics, Universiti Malaya, Malaysia. She attained her PhD from Lancaster University, UK. Her research interests include Media Discourses and Multimodality, focusing specifically upon public discourses in mainstream and social media that relate to public health, migration, terrorism issues. She has been actively involved with Universiti Malaya's social outreach initiatives to offer solutions to the mental health challenges faced by Malaysian during the COVID-19 pandemic (Caring Together/UMPrihatin), focusing specifically on the social media platforms of Telegram and Facebook. She is currently compiling a database of research and data from all over the world to help Malaysian scholars in their research on COVID-19.

Huey Fen Cheong (The managing editor of *COVID-19 in Malaysia* multidisciplinary series) is a Senior Lecturer in the Department of English Language, Faculty of Languages and Linguistics, Universiti Malaya. Her research interests are interdisciplinary from gender studies and linguistics to marketing and psychology. Her works are usually humanitarian, from gender equality (for men and women) and anti-racism (skin whitening and Black Lives Matter) to decolonisation of academia. The last one explains the initiative behind this book series in creating a platform for researchers to study the COVID-19 pandemic in Malaysia, which addresses the lack of COVID-19 research and publication in South East Asia. She is also the founder of the Facebook group, (post-)COVID job market in Malaysia (https://www.facebook.com/groups/2805574166392321), which shares information about the New Normal and the Next Normal of employment and employability during this challenging time.

COVID-19 in Asia

COVID-19, Business, and Economy in Malaysia
Retrospective and Prospective Perspectives
Edited by Weng Marc Lim, Surinderpal Kaur,
and Huey Fen Cheong

COVID-19, Education, and Literacy in Malaysia
Social Contexts of Teaching and Learning
Edited by Ambigapathy Pandian, Surinderpal Kaur,
and Huey Fen Cheong

COVID-19 and Psychology in Malaysia
Psychosocial Effects, Coping, and Resilience
Edited by D. Gerard Joseph Louis, Surinderpal Kaur,
and Huey Fen Cheong

COVID-19, Education, and Literacy in Malaysia

Social Contexts of Teaching and Learning

Edited by
Ambigapathy Pandian,
Surinderpal Kaur,
and Huey Fen Cheong

Routledge
Taylor & Francis Group

LONDON AND NEW YORK

First published 2022
by Routledge
2 Park Square, Milton Park, Abingdon, Oxon OX14 4RN

and by Routledge
605 Third Avenue, New York, NY 10158

Routledge is an imprint of the Taylor & Francis Group, an Informa business

British Library Cataloguing-in-Publication Data
A catalogue record for this book is available from the British Library

Library of Congress Cataloguing-in-Publication Data
A catalog record has been requested for this book

ISBN: 978-1-032-02286-4 (hbk)
ISBN: 978-1-032-02287-1 (pbk)
ISBN: 978-1-003-18273-3 (ebk)

DOI: 10.4324/9781003182733

Typeset in Times
by KnowledgeWorks Global Ltd.

Contents

Figures

Tables

List of contributors

*Arranged according to the alphabetical order of the last names.

Natasya Abdullah is a Medical Lecturer in Pharmacology at the Faculty of Medicine and Health Sciences, Universiti Sains Islam Malaysia (USIM). She graduated with a Medical Degree in 2002 from Universiti Kebangsaan Malaysia (UKM) and later obtained her Masters in Medical Sciences (MMedSc) from the International Islamic University Malaysia (IIUM) in 2010. She also holds a PhD from the University of Nottingham, United Kingdom with specialised in conducting systematic review and meta-analysis. Her research interest consists of pharmacology, natural products as well as medical education.

Muhammad Nizam Awang is a Senior Lecturer in Law at the Faculty of Syariah and Law, Universiti Sains Islam Malaysia. His expertise lies broadly in the area of regulation and governance of new technologies, particularly health law and bioethics; and information and privacy laws. He obtained his PhD from Brunel University where he studied on the implications of public international law and food safety law on nanotechnology products. His current works focus on legal, policy, and ethical implications of technologies associated with automation and digital technologies, artificial intelligence, and robotics.

Tamara Boscia studied Foreign Languages and Literature (master's degree) at the University of Urbino, Italy. Her main field of study was Italian history and literature, English and French language and literature. She specialized in Didactics of Foreign Languages-Learning in L2 (CLIL) at Ca' Foscari University, Venice. She worked as secondary school teacher of English and CLIL (history and geography). She now works in the cultural office of the Italian Embassy in Kuala Lumpur and teaches Italian language and culture at Universiti Malaya. She is interested in research on Foreign Language teaching and learning.

Omar Colombo is Senior Lecturer at Universiti Malaya. He studied Linguistics and Didactics of Foreign Languages. He completed a PhD in Applied Linguistics, specialization in Linguistics and Foreign Languages (University of Grenoble). He taught Italian and French Foreign Languages, translation, linguistics and didactics of the foreign languages. He has worked in three different countries: in France (Universities of Lyon, Grenoble, Chambery and Rennes), in the UAE (Paris-Sorbonne University Abu Dhabi) and in Malaysia (Universiti Malaya). He has been engaged in research and publications in Foreign Language teaching and learning, in comparative language studies and in technology enhanced learning (new technologies).

Ali Jalalian Daghigh is a Senior Lecturer in Faculty of Languages and Linguistics, Universiti Malaya, Malaysia (UM). Prior to joining UM, he was a postdoctoral fellow in English Language Studies at Universiti Sains Malaysia. His research interests lie within (Critical) Discourse Studies, Education as well as Translation Studies. His recent publications have appeared in several international peer reviewed journals including Pedagogy, Culture, and Society, Journal of Asian Englishes, FORUM, inTRAlinea, Journal of Asia Pacific Translation and Intercultural Studies, and Southern African Linguistics and Applied Language Studies.

Prasana Rosaline Fernandez is an Assistant Professor at the Department of Advertising, Xiamen University Malaysia. Her areas of research include risk and health discourse, green marketing, branding, and advertising.

Rodney C. Jubilado is an Associate Professor at the University of Hawaii @ Hilo. He obtained Ph.D. in Theoretical Linguistics from the Universiti Kebangsaan Malaysia in 2010. Multilingual by nature and speaks fluent English, Bahasa Malaysia, Filipino, Cebuano, and Spanish. His research areas are contemporary general linguistics and historical linguistics.

Sheena Kaur is a Senior Lecturer at the Faculty of Languages and Linguistics, Universiti Malaya. She obtained her PhD in Applied Linguistics from Lancaster University, U.K. Her main research interests are corpus linguistics, sociolinguistics as well as social sciences studies related to covid-19. Her recent publication includes a commentary "The coronavirus pandemic in Malaysia" published in the WOS-indexed journal of Psychological Trauma: Theory, Research, Practice, and Policy.

Komalata Manokaran has been a freelance tutor since 2010. She received a degree in Education (Bachelor in Teaching English as Second Language) from the Management and Science University (MSU) in 2012 and obtained a Master's Degree in Linguistics from the Universiti Malaya (UM) in 2020. Her current research interests include morphology studies in blending, advertising language, and pragmatic.

Devika Nadarajah is a faculty member at Putra Business School (PBS). She holds a doctorate degree in Business Process Management (Quality Management) from Universiti Malaya. She has a master's degree in Quality and Productivity Improvement and bachelor's degree in Statistics from University Kebangsaan Malaysia. She is the Manager of Quality Assurance – responsible for quality and accreditation at PBS. She teaches Business Research Methods and Operations Management for MBA and Research Methodology for PhD. Her research is centred on quality and supply chain management. Prior to academia, Devika served in the IT and telecommunications industry for over 10 years.

Liap-Teck Ong is a Lecturer attached with the Faculty of Business, Design and Arts, Swinburne University, Sarawak Campus. His research focuses on second-career academics, business education, authentic learning, and bridging of academia with industry. Leveraging on his extensive work experience across industrial sectors and geographical boundaries before joining academia, he coordinates industry consulting projects that connects students with the business. At the faculty, he teaches capstone unit and international business.

Shyi Nian Ong is a Senior Lecturer of Japanese Language and Linguistics at the Faculty of Languages and Linguistics, Universiti Malaya. He obtained Ph.D. in Applied Comparative Linguistics from the University Putra Malaysia in 2021. His research interest areas are loanwords, the morphology of Malay and Japanese, and translations.

Noor Dzuhaidah Osman is a Senior Lecturer in Law at the Faculty of Syariah and Law, Universiti Sains Islam Malaysia (USIM). She is a graduate of Bachelor of Laws (LLB) of Sheffield Hallam University.

She pursued her PhD at Nottingham Law School, Nottingham Trent University, United Kingdom. She presented her research interests in environmental biosafety, bioethics, food security and law, technology and regulation, sociology and law, media and law, and international environmental law to various audiences including Vladivostok State University of Economics and Service (VSUES), Russia, Jenderal Soedirman University (UNSOED), Indonesia and Sultan Sharif Ali Islamic University (UNISSA), Brunei.

Zairina A Rahman is a Medical Lecturer at the Faculty of Medicine and Health Sciences, Universiti Sains Islam Malaysia. She obtained her degree in medicine (MD, Universiti Kebangsaan Malaysia). After graduated with Master of Public Health (University of Malaya) and Master of Public Health (Occupational) (University of Malaya) she worked at the Diseases Control Division, Ministry of Health Malaysia as Public Health Specialist. Apart from teaching public health and research methodology to the medical students in USIM, she also delivers lectures/talks at National Institute for Occupational Safety and Health (NIOSH), Ministry of Health Malaysia and to the community.

Thilaga Ravinthar is an English Language Teacher at Universiti Pendidikan Sultan Idris. She graduated with first class degree in TESL (UPSI) and has served various schools before commencing work in UPSI in 2014. She has experience of teaching English for students of various ages and regions. Her key interests include teaching and learning English for ESL learners and studying the problems faced by students in the learning the language. She has obtained her Masters of Arts in Linguistics and her area of specialization is Discourse Analysis.

Khursiah Mohd Sauffi is an English Language Teacher at the Centre for Languages and General Studies, Universiti Pendidikan Sultan Idris (UPSI). She has taught a number of English Proficiency courses for local undergraduates and international students since 2014. She has obtained her Master's Degree in Teaching English as a Second Language (M.Ed TESL).

Edmund Ui-Hang Sim has a PhD (Biochemistry) from the University of Queensland (Australia) and a Bachelor of Science (Hons) in Genetics from the University of Malaya (Malaysia). Dr Sim is currently a Professor of Molecular Biology (specialization in Cancer Genetics) at the Faculty of Resource Science and Technology at the Universiti Malaysia Sarawak, where he teaches Bioinformatics,

Medical Biotechnology, and Research Methodology. He has been an academic and researcher since 1994 and has published in cancer biology and genetics, biochemistry, gene therapy, microbiology, public health, cancer risk studies, bioethics, and public perception of biomedical sciences.

Su-Hie Ting has a PhD (Applied Linguistics) from the University of Queensland, a Master's of Science (Teaching of English as a Second Language) from Universiti Putra Malaysia and a Bachelor of Arts (Hons) from Universiti Sains Malaysia. She teaches research methodology at the Faculty of Language and Communication, Universiti Malaysia Sarawak. She has published on communication strategies, language choice and identity, academic writing, and health risk communication.

Nur Syazana Umar is a lecturer in Community Health at Faculty of Nursing and Allied Health Science, Lincoln University College. She holds a PhD in Science and Technology from Faculty of Medicine and Health Sciences, Islamic Science University Malaysia (USIM) with specialised in community health. She obtained a master degree from the National University of Malaysia (UKM) in Community Health Sciences majoring in Epidemiology and Medical statistics. She is also a certified Registered Nurse (RN) and holds a Bachelor of Nursing from International Islamic University (IIUM).

Preface

The times of the coronavirus disease (COVID-19) are difficult, confusing, and stressful. The focus on literacy and education is important to open new learning choices and opportunities. Literacy is a force for inclusion and resilience to reimagine how we live, learn, and perform activities, especially when we witness closures of education institutions, changing role of educators, uncertainties in learning settings, and making appropriate health decisions. The rapid rush and push for digital technologies press us all to react and respond to new literacy experiences that shape people's learning, safety, and the quality of wellbeing.

This book entitled *"COVID-19, Education and Literacy in Malaysia: Social Contexts of Teaching and Learning"* addresses some of the points of intersection where diverse communities of learners explore unprecedented disruption, learn to grow through challenges and craft new resources for advancing the interests and capabilities of learners. The book aims to take us further and deeper into reflecting the learning essentials of our pandemic times. Much of the studies presented here explore teaching and learning matters from January 2020 till December 2020 amidst the pandemic when educators, learners, and other experts grappled with problems and solutions to present rapid action for the literacy and education context. This collection brings together educators, language, and health scholars to discuss the investigations they have begun about the nature of education and literacy, technology, the growing complexity and ambiguity surrounding knowledge, and perception on health and wellness in responding to the challenges of new learning.

The first section, *"The New Normal: Online Teaching and Learning with COVID-19"* offers Chapter 1 to Chapter 4 that delve into online learning experiences of university students; the second section, *"Corona Speak: Issues in Language and Literacy"* carries Chapters 5 and 6 that explore expressive and word features in the language domain while the final section, *"Flattening the Curve: Matters on Health Literacy"* presents Chapters 7 and 8 that deliberate on the capacity to understand basic health knowledge to make well-informed decisions.

Chapter 1 on *International students and learning experiences in higher education* by Sheena Kaur, Prasana Rosaline Fernandez, and Ali Jalalian Daghigh highlights views from international students who brave pandemic challenges to confront academic, administrative, social, financial, and emotional challenges. The voices of students on the need to use a variety of technologies to support learning, creating flexible fee structures to address financial woes, and addressing psychological disorders such as stress, depression, and insomnia help the higher education industry stakeholders to strengthen the learning experiences of international students.

Chapter 2 on *University students' online learning in Capstone Unit* by Liap-Teck Ong enables educators to reflect on better teaching and learning strategies, specifically in encouraging students to develop skills in working with business partners on online platforms. His study unveils both productive and challenging students' experiences that will facilitate the online delivery of Capstone units in the new normal.

Chapter 3 on *Online assessments for university students: A case study of a business school* by

Devika Nadarajah considers the shift from traditional assessments to online assessments, which involved changes in examination modes and question formats. She argues that the case-studies analysis approach in the final examinations were able to sustain the quality and efficacy of student learning outcome assessments.

Chapter 4 on *Video log (Vlog) for enhancing speaking skills in the ESL Classroom* by Thilaga Ravinthar and Khursiah Mohd Sauffi ascertains that the video log (Vlog) can be perceived as an alternative learning tool in teaching speaking skills. Their work establishes that students felt positive and productive as they were able to cooperate and make good decisions in topic selection, learning technical skills, peer evaluations on their practices in speaking skills, and in interacting with their instructors in a very testing time.

Chapter 5 on *Foreign language learning at the university: Students' perceptions and emotions* by Omar Colombo and Tamara Boscia focus on learners' perceptions and emotions of a distance learning course in a Malaysian university, during the COVID-19 emergency. The learners' main concerns were related to the clear feeling of frustration caused by Internet connection and computer disruption, but this did not affect learners' foreign language learning motivation. The authors, however, assert that interpersonal interaction in the e-learning environment and online face-to-face engagement was important when giving continuous constructive feedback to students on their learning activities.

Chapter 6 on *A morphological analysis of COVID-19 novel words used in Malaysia* by Komalata Manokaran, Shyi Nian Ong, and Rodney C. Jubilado centres on the morphological analysis of newly coined words during COVID-19 and the meaning of the words. It is interesting to note that while struggling with the ongoing pandemic, the authors affirm that the words like lockdown, MySejahtera, and Selangkah used during the outbreak were mostly coined by compounding.

Chapter 7 on *Public knowledge and perception of COVID-19 and its preventive measures* by Edmund Ui-Hang Sim and Su-Hie Ting investigated perceived knowledge of COVID-19 disease and perceived effectiveness of preventive measures among Malaysians. The analysis of survey data revealed that the public believed that they have moderate knowledge of COVID-19 disease. They note that individuals with good health literacy are more likely to take preventive measures and seek treatment if they fall sick.

Chapter 8 on *Knowledge, attitude, and practice on health and legal measures* by Natasya Abdullah, Noor Dzuhaidah Osman, Nur Syazana Umar, Muhammad Nizam Awang, and Zairina A Rahman reiterate that health communication and policies need baseline information on people's knowledge, attitudes, and practices with regard to the COVID-19 pandemic. The authors note that a majority of the study respondents expressed their willingness to adhere to the government's prevention and control measures for the well-being of their families.

Navigating through the COVID-19 crisis and its aftermath demands strength as we confront disruption in literacy and education. This book takes stock of some of the difficulties encountered by diverse learning communities while adapting to online knowledge cultures to understand how we can improve our learning and wellbeing systems. In literacy as in health, we are safe when our communities are safe; we prosper when everyone in our communities prosper too.

The editors would like to acknowledge the ideas and hard work put forward by everyone involved in this book. The contributors responded readily when we asked them to review, update, and expand their original chapters with only a few months to complete this work. We hope that you, the reader, will find this book useful, stimulating, and inspiring.

Ambigapathy Pandian
Surinderpal Kaur
Huey Fen Cheong

Part A

The new normal: Online teaching and learning with COVID-19

1 International students and learning experiences in higher education

Sheena Kaur, Prasana Rosaline Fernandez, and Ali Jalalian Daghigh

1.1 Introduction

International students form a vital part of the higher education community in Malaysia. They are key drivers to the country's knowledge-based economy, and they make a significant contribution to revenue generation. Malaysia ranks one of the top ten destinations in the world for international students (Executive Summary of the Malaysia Education Blueprint 2015–2025 for Higher Education). The outbreak of the COVID-19 pandemic, however, has dramatically impacted higher education globally subjecting universities to a range of challenges.

Higher education is now facing a new challenge in sustaining student enrolment as interest in studying abroad significantly decreases with students cancelling their plans to study abroad (Mok et al., 2021). The pandemic has raised concerns among international students about the uncertainty of their future. It is important that they are supported, and the enrolments can be sustained under the current scenario in order to continue providing quality education and strengthening the overall positive learning experience. Hence, in supporting the welfare of international students, universities have to make sure they provide safe and welcoming environments and look after the health, safety, and well-being of their international students. In this context, the study addresses the following research questions:

1 What challenges do the international students at the higher education institutions in Malaysia face during the COVID-19 outbreak?
2 What are the recommendations of the stakeholders to address the challenges faced by the international students to cope with the COVID-19 outbreak?

DOI: 10.4324/9781003182733-2

1.2 Literature review

The COVID-19 pandemic has raised unprecedented challenges around the world, affecting numerous industries including higher education. Several studies have explored from different standpoints the impact of COVID-19 on both local and international students and the various challenges it has posed to them globally and locally (Aristovnik et al., 2020; Blackmore, 2020; Demuyakor, 2020; Firang, 2020; Gallagher et al., 2020; Misirlis et al., 2020; Mok et al., 2021; Morris et al., 2020; Nguyen and Balakrishnan, 2020; Peters et al., 2020; Sahu, 2020; Schulmann, 2020; Sundarasen et al., 2020). The following sections present a review of these studies.

1.2.1 Global studies

Previous studies have highlighted three main reasons for these challenges. The first reason is the rapid transition to the online mode of teaching. Aristovnik et al.'s (2020) study showed that problems such as deficient computer skills and high workload were the main challenges the students were facing. By surveying the Ghanaian students in China, Demuyakor (2020) found out that these students struggled with inconvenient internet access as well as network disruption for attending online classes. In another study in Russia, Novikov (2020), through a survey with international students, identified several shortcomings in the new online mode of instruction including difficulties in using technology, decrease in teacher-student interaction, fatigue, and demotivation.

The second main reason for the challenges is the movement restriction as reported in some studies (Martel, 2020; Mok et al., 2021; Sahu, 2020). For instance, Mok et al. (2021), surveying international students in China and Hong Kong, mentioned that many students changed or cancelled their education plans due to travel restrictions and campus closure. Martel (2020) reported that in the US, many university departments and campuses were closed, and international students' travels were cancelled.

Several studies have also shown that many international students face financial issues due to the loss of their jobs, support of their families, or cancellation of their university funding (e.g. in Australia, Gallagher et al., 2020; Morris et al., 2020; Nguyen and Balakrishnan, 2020; in Canada Firang, 2020). For instance, Gallagher et al. (2020) remarked that a large number of international students in Australia were in severe need of financial assistance to handle their food and accommodation.

As the result of the above-mentioned issues as well as other matters such as the chronic stress of the pandemic and the students' concern about their families, several studies have reported mental, emotional, and physical health disorders among students (in Australia, Gallagher et al., 2020; in the Netherlands, Misirlis et al., 2020; in China, Peters et al., 2020).

Previous studies, while limited in number, have addressed the reasons behind international students' challenges under the COVID-19 pandemic. This is a necessary step in identifying the international students' specific problems. However, to date, little attention has been paid to the possible solutions to the identified challenges. Martel's (2020) study on the effects of COVID-19 on education and students in the US merely reported the financial aids such as application fee waiver, deferment of tuition fees, and emergency funds provided by the universities. In his study on the impact of the COVID-19 pandemic on international students in Canada, Firang (2020) made some recommendations on how social workers can support vulnerable international students by identifying the underlying political and social structures that discriminate against international students in the Canadian society; connecting international students to community resources and support; providing information and resources to raise awareness about international students' vulnerable conditions and finally campaigning to persuade governments to pursue social justice for international students in Canada. It is noticeable that the top-down suggestions made by both studies are context-specific and limited in generalizability to other contexts.

1.2.2 *Local studies*

In the Malaysian context, there is a lack of research on international students' experiences under the COVID-19 pandemic. Most of these studies were conducted quantitatively through the use of online surveys and focused on aspects of e-learning and psychological impacts. A study on the impact of COVID-19 on local students conducted by Sundarasen et al. (2020), centred on the causes of the students' psychological problems due to COVID-19. The results from the online survey showed that some predominant stressors are financial constraints, online learning, uncertainty related to their academic performance, and future career prospects. Another study by Selvanathan et al. (2020) also used online surveys to examine the experiences of students from private and public universities with online learning during the pandemic, and the findings revealed that students were dissatisfied with the delivery of online teaching and learning initiatives.

Additionally, Wan Mohd Yunus et al. (2021) used Qualtrics in their study to analyse the impact of COVID-19 lockdown on Malaysian tertiary students and the findings showed that the lockdown had a significant negative impact on their emotional well-being, happiness, and work-life balance. Similarly, Yassin et al. (2021) examined the psychological impact of local and international students in universities in Malaysia through a survey conducted on 219 students. The results highlighted that the outbreak of COVID-19 caused psychological stress that made online learning less effective and less helpful for students. Al-Kumaim's et al. (2021) study on the impact of online learning on Malaysian tertiary students produced similar results as the findings reiterated the daunting stress factors faced by the students such as information and work overload, long solitary hours spent in front of computers, and the lack of motivation. The findings also revealed the lack of preparedness by both the universities and the students in dealing with the new normal.

This research used a mixed-mode method: content analysis on the literature on COVID-19 and an online survey on 486 students. Finally, Nasir et al. (2021) looked at the impact of COVID-19 pandemic on academic survival among postgraduate students in Malaysia. The online survey conducted on 606 postgraduate students highlighted firstly, academic adversities as a result of online learning, secondly, the financial stress because of lack of funding, and thirdly, the lack of social relationships since social interaction was curtailed. The findings from all the studies concurred on the urgency of appropriate strategies being implemented to relieve the students' pressing psychological, financial, and social problems.

Therefore, the present study serves to address this gap via focus group interviews and, more importantly, propose some solutions to tackle the international students' challenges through a bottom-up analysis. To this end, the study takes a qualitative approach to delve into the experiences of international students studying at two universities in Malaysia.

1.3 Method

Data collection via focus group interviews and background of the respondents are described in this section.

1.3.1 Focus group interviews

The study uses focus group interviews to collect qualitative insights from a purposive sample of participants into the challenges faced by the international students and recommended solutions to cope with the challenges. Focus group interview is a method which is commonly used in exploratory studies. Morgan (1996, p. 130) defines focus groups as "a research technique that collects data through group interaction on a topic determined by the researcher". The target population for this research was international students as well as administrative and academic staff members from a public and a private university in Malaysia.

In order to connect to the international students, the International Student Centre of the respondents' universities collaborated to provide the researchers with the students' contact details. The study also used a snowball technique to approach the international students. In this regard, *WhatsApp* groups were formed both for undergraduate and postgraduate international students to disseminate the call for focus group interviews participation, and after the final selection of the participants, the invitation link for the interviews was sent on students' emails via *Google Meet*.

Focus group interviews were conducted online on *Google Meet* from October 2020 to January 2021 separately among the students, academics, and management officers of a public and private university in Malaysia. A list of questions was designed and used as a guide to prompt the participants and to elicit answers. The questions posed to the students were related to the challenges they faced and how they overcame them, their concerns, and the effect of the outbreak. For the administrators and academic staff members, the questions touched on the major concerns and challenges of the students during the lockdown, the support provided by the university and solutions to the problems faced by the students. The researchers concluded that saturation has been reached after interviewing a total of 28 students, 7 administrative, and 5 academic staff.

1.3.2 Respondent background

Out of the 28 students, 19 were undergraduates and 9 were postgraduate students. Fourteen of the participants were males and 13 were females. The postgraduate students were from various countries such as India, Bangladesh, Saudi Arabia, Nigeria, Kyrgyzstan, Pakistan, and Japan. They were both Master's and PhD students in the sciences, social sciences, and arts and humanities. The undergraduate group participants came from Nepal, Bangladesh, Sri Lanka, Pakistan, China, India, South Africa (British citizenship), Indonesia, China, and Albania. The faculties they were attached to were the sciences (Faculty of Engineering) and arts (Business and Accountancy; Arts and Social Sciences). Participation of the university management officers for the focus group interviews consists of two officers and five academic staff from the private university; and from the public university, the officers came from the International Student Services Unit (3), a Residential College (1), and the Visa Unit (1).

1.4 Findings

Responses from the participants were all transcribed and grouped thematically for analysis. Four main themes emerged from the focus group discussions and these centred on ordeals faced by the students, namely academic challenges, financial challenges, social and personal well-being challenges, as well as administrative challenges. The participants also posed possible solutions to these challenges as the pandemic is here for the long haul.

1.4.1 Academic challenges

COVID-19 has drastically changed the educational landscape posing unique challenges to international students. The international students, academics, and management officers echoed similar academic difficulties faced by international students whether residing in Malaysia or in their home countries.

1.4.1.1 Online teaching and learning

The new norm of online teaching and learning which required students to listen to online lectures, conduct online presentations, and attempt online tests and examinations proved to be too taxing and uninteresting: *"The biggest challenge was to adapt to online learning, online presentations and online meetings ... they are all unfamiliar to me"*; *"In class, I usually participate ... to make the class as interesting as possible. But now, I rather sleep or use my phone because it has become extremely boring"*; *"... lecturers are really having a hard time with us because they really don't know how to make things interesting for us"*.

This frustration was fuelled by the lack of communication and interaction as online lectures, class activities, and hands-on practical skill-based lessons had insufficient physical face-to-face interaction between lecturers and students, and similarly students with their peers. A student highlighted that most of the time the lecturers kept their webcams off, so, there was an absence of eye contact which made lectures less effective. Similar comments were repeated by other students: *"Because of COVID-19, the physical classes have become online and the online learning may be sometimes inefficient for me because we cannot see our lecturers face-to-face ..."; "... now it is easy to become lazy ... you know ... while studying at home ... I have to rely more on myself and we cannot discuss my problems with my classmates and lecturers"*.

The academics agreed that online classes are less interactive and engaging: *"Most of them are not interested in listening to our pre-recorded lecture 100% ... they are not willing to talk to me ... so, I forced them to talk to me"*. This was attributed to the students' lack of preparedness and discipline in coping with online classes. Likewise, students expressed feeling bored as sitting in front of a computer for an extended period of time listening to online lectures was monotonous and triggered loss of concentration and focus. The students wanted more interesting content besides PowerPoints on newer interactive platforms: *"... just listening to you and looking at your PowerPoint slides is very boring. Can you share with us ... for example video links?"*

1.4.1.2 Time differences

There were also concerns about time differences from international students residing outside Malaysia. They highlighted the difficulties in attempting group assignments as connecting with their peers was demanding due to different time zones. Additionally, they faced problems scheduling research meetings and consultations, attending online classes, and attempting tests according to Malaysian time. An academic commented: *"... because of the time difference my student deferred taking the module"*.

1.4.1.3 Information technology (IT) facilities

The universities were unprepared for this pandemic and as such there were issues related to IT infrastructure and accessibility of university resources that hampered online teaching and learning. Students faced internet disruption and the unavailability of IT equipment. Besides, students working on research and those enrolled in IT and design courses required specific software. They faced hurdles in accessing the universities' free software or obtaining subscriptions via online portals while studying from their home countries. Due to the inaccessibility of online library resources, students struggled in conducting online searches and downloading research materials. This was confirmed by the academics and management officers: "*... some students faced difficulty while carrying out their assignments, uploading the files on Moodle, downloading study materials, purchasing or getting subscriptions and installing software from online sources*". Similarly, students could not access university resources like the studios and computer labs for practical assignments in photography and advertising courses.

The postgraduate students faced additional obstacles as they encountered difficulties in collecting data and accessing the computer, library, and science labs which are vital for the completion of their research. A student disclosed: "*I came to Malaysia on 4th of March, 2020, ... after fifteen days there was a lockdown ... So, I came back to India again ... I want to collect data in Delhi, but due to COVID-19, the colleges and schools are closed so I can't get the data easily*". The students were also not allowed to use the campus facilities during the initial lockdown but later under the movement control order, the universities allowed on-campus postgraduate students to use the labs for critical research work. However, the students complained that obtaining timely approval from their respective faculties to access these labs was a struggle because of the lockdown and movement control order, and this slowed their progress: "*When the lock down happened, I was still in Malaysia ... We all were forbidden to go into the university lab ... it was the main source of stress for me because I'm in Malaysia ... and I can't defer my studies ... my progress slowed down. There is no access to the labs, nothing*".

1.4.1.4 Proposed solutions

To mitigate the academic challenges, the participants concurred that traditional teaching methods were not appropriate for online classes. Lecturer-student communication needed to be enhanced by integrating technology effectively for a better learning experience and for ensuring students graduate on time. The participants agreed that various platforms and software for recording of lectures, sharing resources, online collaboration, and creating virtual laboratories should be made available for seamless learning. Students wanted more interactive and synchronous platforms like live video streaming, the ability to share screens as well as text chat field to make the classes interesting: "*They should change the way of teaching … like … they should be more interactive with us …*"; "*I was hoping if we can implement like YouTube tutorials …*".

The participants maintained that more lecturer-student *WhatsApp/ WeChat* groups should be formed for timely notification of academic activities. They explained that these platforms allowed discussions and aid in getting more timely feedback from their lecturers. They also wished lecturers would keep their webcam on while delivering pre-recorded lectures as it made the lessons more interactive: "*… like keeping the camera on … so that we [can] actually see them and [do not] feel not so isolated*". Additionally, both the students and academics agreed that there should be more live online classes rather than pre-recorded lectures as it facilitates real-time learning and instils discipline: "*I found that if I deliver my lectures live, it works better than pre-recorded lectures … I can see my job done in a very effective manner*".

The students wanted the problem of internet connectivity on campus to be resolved with upgraded online connectivity and speed. For better access to IT infrastructure, the students proposed that the university launched a Rental Laptops Programme. They felt this would address the problem of inaccessibility of computer labs and software for research, IT, and design courses.

1.4.2 Financial challenges

A significant theme that emerged from the focus groups was the financial constraints faced by foreign students. The pandemic had a profound effect on the global economy and this affected most of the students tremendously.

1.4.2.1 Loss of financial support

The students in the study spoke about the difficulties in paying fees as their families in their home countries were distraught with the loss of income as a result of nationwide lockdowns. Following the widespread outbreak of COVID-19, global volatility spiked and as a result, postgraduate students were faced with cancellation of scholarships by their funding agency. Suddenly, students found themselves in highly precarious financial and living situations struggling to pay their tuition fees, their rent, and their daily living expenses: "*… I will not be able to afford to live here because there is no scholarship, no*

RA grant or RA money"; "*… it is very expensive to order food through Grab so I eat sausages and eggs most of the time. I don't tell my parents about it*".

1.4.2.2 Difficulty securing employment

Paid work is important for these international students but now they are faced with two major concerns. Firstly, the economic impact has made it difficult for them to secure financial assistance from the faculty or the university through research assistantship or monthly stipend for PhD student survival. Secondly, there are limited or no opportunities for them to secure employment outside the university campus due to strict immigration laws: "*Now I started to look for a job … so I can help my parents to pay my tuition fees and it is extremely hard for an international student to look for a job in this country … we have a student visa so it is difficult to work here*".

1.4.2.3 Proposed solutions

The participants from the management team confirmed that steps have been taken to ease the financial burden of both the international and local students during this pandemic. They revealed that special funding from the government was awarded to universities to deal with the COVID-19 crisis. Free food and recreational funds were provided to students on campus in the initial phase of the movement control order. Semester deferment and postponing options were also offered to the students to reduce their financial burden: "*We had a student from India whose parents' business was affected by the pandemic … we advised him to defer the semester so that the parents in that duration of deferment can go on a monthly instalment payment until next year. So that when he comes back, his account is free from debt*". Nevertheless, the management team suggested that there should be more fund allocation for the students to deal with emergency situations during the pandemic.

The students suggested that employment opportunities for international students should be created on campus as the Malaysian Immigration laws are strict on international students working on a student visa. They said this would not only give them the much-needed additional income but it would also beef up their resumes for future employment: "*I would love to work at UM as it is a place where international students want to work … . I would like something that I can write in my CV … that means something when I apply for a real job after I graduate*"; "*... if the university can help me find a job, ... I need to work to get money, it would be nice if the university can recommend a few places ... and have a collaboration with a few companies ... that would be helpful*". The postgraduate students also suggested monthly stipends to be allocated to them through research assistant positions from grants.

1.4.3 Challenges on social and personal well-being

The academic, financial, and social pressures along with the chronic stress of the pandemic created mental, emotional, and physical health problems. The students shared their anxiety and fear of being cooped up either in hostels on campus or in homes in their own countries.

1.4.3.1 Travel restrictions

The ban on travelling had a profound effect on them as it disrupted their recreational and educational trips. It also disrupted their travelling plans whether travelling to other countries for exchange programmes or visiting their home countries. The lockdown and lack of interaction made them feel imprisoned: "*... we are stuck on campus here, it is very boring, we hang out with the same friends, we eat the same food, we hang out in the same place, we do the same thing every day, it is very frustrating ...*". The boredom, routine, and frustration have contributed to stress, lethargy, and sleep deprivation: "*I am physically okay, but I am mentally tired, so, it's a bit hard to sleep at night.*"

1.4.3.2 Social isolation

The participants agreed that long periods of self-isolation could have an adverse impact on the psychological well-being of students. There were also incidences of depression and suicidal thoughts among international students: "*... they miss home, they are bored, and coping with online learning is just too much for them ...*". Dealing with students' suicidal thoughts was challenging for the management team: "*... they even write that they want to commit suicide ... we try to track and see who they are and we try to give them extra attention ...*"; "*... our main priority was not to allow them to go into depression, because it affects their families back home ...*". The students felt physically isolated because of the restrictions on face-to-face socialization and social gatherings. This social isolation and loneliness contributed to the students' deteriorating physical, emotional, and mental health.

1.4.3.3 Restrictions on recreational activities

The closure of the gymnasium and sports facilities aggravated the problem as the students were denied physical fitness activities that they once enjoyed. It also contributed to eating disorders: *"I have an eating disorder, hyper gymnasia and so the gyms were closed at that time. If you do have hyper gymnasia ... you over exercise constantly to control your calorie intakes. So the gym was closed, so I had to find a different format of exercise, but I couldn't walk, I couldn't run outside ...".*

1.4.3.4 Proposed solutions

The management team clarified that campus activities with strict standard operating guidelines were allowed in the later part of the control movement order. Reduced number of students was permitted to take part in open-air games like badminton and small group activities at residential colleges with social distancing. The students proposed that there should be more online recreational events organised for the international student community. They recommended clubs to be established to initiate virtual fun oriented and social activities. They highlighted podcasting to be a good way to share folk tales, childhood memories, music, and recipes among international students to enjoy cultural diversity: *"You can do podcasting ... have discussion sessions where you sit in a group ... you just have fun you know ... weekly a club just gets together ... the university really does not encourage anything like that".*

The management team confirmed that mitigation strategies like group support and counselling services at the campus were in place to deal with the personal well-being of the students: *"... we have a team of wardens here to support the students. We have counseling so at any point they need help we personally assist them ...".* The management team assured that universities are taking measures to prevent, identify, and deal with the mental health problems of international students and that student well-being during this pandemic is their priority.

1.4.4 Administrative challenges

Besides the academic, financial, and social well-being challenges faced by the students, they also expressed their frustrations with several administrative challenges. The most notable concern was to do with the visa.

1.4.4.1 Delay in getting visas

The visa unit plays a critical role for international students as it manages the renewal of student and dependent passes and it also acts as a liaison for communication and documentation with external agencies. Hence, the closure of the visa unit in the university added to the students' frustration as it meant delays in getting their passes renewed. Students with families had to produce bank balance statements of RM10,000 in order to obtain dependent passes. This is extremely exasperating for them, who often only have a short window of time in which to get their visa sorted out: "*... it's my dependent pass. I have a daughter with me here, she attends international school. I had to renew my dependent pass... I had a very serious problem.... (EMGS) they require some documents and I had to submit again and again and I had to visit the Embassy of Japan in Kuala Lumpur ...*". In addition, the students touched on the lack of prompt response during emergencies when verification of student status is required at the police station or for legal matters.

1.4.4.2 Difficulty in opening bank account

The international students who joined the university during the pandemic encountered difficulties in opening bank accounts due to the lockdown and movement control order in the initial stages. This was an additional burden to them as the majority were already facing financial troubles due to the pandemic. As a result, the students were unable to have money transferred to pay their tuition fees, bills, and monthly expenses. Furthermore, they could not make online purchases of goods and services which were unavoidably necessary due to the pandemic.

1.4.4.3 Proposed solutions

The students proposed for the visa unit to be accessible to them during this crucial period to assist with procedural problems for visa renewal/extension or verification in a timely manner. They suggested that the university develops its own tracking system for international students' visa applications to ensure speedy and smooth processing: "*If they let us submit the soft copies online the problem can be solved*". Another suggestion was for an effective communication and integrated approach to be implemented for crisis management of the COVID-19 situation. They recommended a university-wide online COVID-19 service centre with a central repository containing standard operating procedures, crisis management, and task force operations for handling complaints and enquiries. The management team supported this proposal: *"I think the way forward would be to put together a central repository in UM website ... all the information related to COVID, it must be made clear to the students and the students can refer to especially when they need help with access to mental support or with access to IT support, academic support, and so on"*. The participants agreed that ultimately the COVID-19 crisis might retrospectively be viewed as an opportunity for universities to strategically revamp systems and prepare for the challenges ahead.

1.5 Discussion

According to the results of the study, the major challenges that the students faced were related to academic, financial, social, and personal well-being and administration.

1.5.1 Academic challenges

The academic challenges were mainly due to the shifts in the mode of instruction to online classes. This included lack of infrastructure at universities, students' inadequate IT knowledge, and inaccessibility of academic resources which were previously addressed in research on international students in different countries (Aristovnik et al., 2020; Demuyakor, 2020; Novikov, 2020). As an immediate solution, students proposed designing IT-based courses and using the Rental Laptop Programme in which they could temporarily use universities' laptops for research with necessary software installed. Inaccessibility to other resources such as libraries and laboratories, whether due to lockdown or delayed permission, was also considered a constraint in students' study plans. They proposed using online platforms to share resources as well as creating and attending virtual laboratories.

In addition to these challenges, the interviewees complained about the quality of online classes due to the lack of interactive activities and the boring nature of one-way instruction by the lecturers which de-motivated the students to follow the courses. Students stated that some of these issues can be managed provided lecturers do not stick to the conventional mode of instruction in an online platform and use a variety of technologies such as multi-functional video streaming platforms allowing all participants a chance to interact. They also recommended extensive use of social media for sharing resources and receiving feedback and notifications. It was also noticeable that the students outside Malaysia with different time zones found the online class hours inappropriate and inconvenient; hence, they preferred using pre-recorded lessons or more flexible class hours. This study also suggests specific plans to improve the quality of online instruction based on students' feedback. These include holding workshops for training lecturers on online teaching initiatives and techniques. In addition, it was suggested that universities provide digital platforms, and new user-friendly curricula with flexible hours to meet the students' needs.

1.5.2 Financial challenges

As for the financial challenge, the results of the study confirmed previous studies on international students (Firang, 2020; Gallagher et al., 2020; Morris et al., 2020; Nasir et al., 2021, Nguyen and Balakrishnan, 2020). Although funds were eventually made available to international students for food and other facilities, the students claimed that they were still under financial pressure as many of them lost their source of income. The management team agreed that these students needed more funds and flexible fee structure to address their financial woes. On the other hand, students suggested that universities could provide them with paid job opportunities on campus as long as the Malaysian immigration law prohibits the employment of international students during the pandemic.

1.5.3 Social and personal well-being challenges

Psychological disorders such as stress, depression, and insomnia due to the lockdown were reported by the interviewees. Similar mental health problems were highlighted by international students in other studies conducted in Malaysia (Al-Kumaim et al., 2021; Wan Mohd Yunus et al., 2021), Australia (Gallagher et al., 2020), the Netherlands (Misirlis et al., 2020), China (Peters et al., 2020), and many other countries (Aristovnik et al., 2020). The management team proposed taking measures such as offering on-campus counselling services, open-air activities, and games. However, the students expressed that universities could take advantage of cyberspace by arranging virtual recreational activities and meetings, as a plausible and affordable solution. This implies that universities should rely on collateral value rather than solely top-down decision-making policies. Respecting the students' viewpoints could create a strong sense of support and connection with the administration. This, and other supportive and recreational activities, can be implemented through social media to reduce the students' sense of loneliness and anxiety.

1.5.4 Administrative challenges

Finally, administrative challenges such as inconveniences in visa renewals and opening of bank accounts were mentioned by some of the students. Likewise, slow processing of students' applications for fee refunds, or course withdrawal aggravated their anxiety and financial distress. The students were particularly dissatisfied with the communication platforms which were not only slow but also restricted to the Malay language, halting students' access to timely and pertinent information. The students recommended that universities develop a special administrative unit to speed up the process. They also requested that the English language be used as the medium of instruction and communication in all websites and platforms. In particular, the interviewees proposed that universities be more flexible and receptive to students' needs and concerns.

1.6 Conclusion

The deteriorating impacts of the pandemic on (higher) education, and in particular, on international students, have already been addressed across the world. The emphasis on attracting international students as the key drivers to the higher education economy and internationalisation in Malaysia motivated researchers to look into international students' experiences during the COVID-19 pandemic. Analysis of focus group interviews with international students, administrative, and academic staff yielded four categories of challenges that international students faced: academic, financial, social and personal well-being, and administrative challenges. Some possible solutions to address these challenges were also elicited from the interviewees.

The findings of this study can provide the relevant stakeholders with insights to better understand and address the challenges that international students face in Malaysia. This is especially important in sustaining the long-term goals of the Malaysian higher education industry in attracting international students. While the present study addressed the core challenges and possible solutions to the impacts of the pandemic on higher education in Malaysia, further studies can be conducted by involving higher-rank stakeholders including relevant agencies and ministries. As the current study is limited to two universities, comparative research could also be done on a larger scale between the various institutions locally and abroad to see if similar challenges exist and how these issues are being dealt with. Further quantitative research can complement the findings of this study by focusing on the relationships among several demographic characteristics such as gender, age, nationality, study level, and marital status.

Post-COVID-19 realities and possibilities

In spite of the challenges, the reality of online teaching and learning as a result of COVID-19 pandemic will continue to make education more and more accessible and flexible. The convenience of remote learning is increasing international students' opportunities to get themselves enrolled without any residential requirement in the host countries. Therefore, while universities need to continue looking into the needs of their international students to sustain a knowledge-based economy, they may need to embark on new strategies to attract international students in the post-COVID-19 era. Also, by drawing on their experiences of COVID-19 opportunities and challenges, they will be able to tackle probable future crises and empower the overall positive learning experience of (international) students.

Acknowledgement

The study is funded by Universiti Malaya COVID-19 Related Special Research Grant (UMCSRG) 2020-2021, Project Account Number CSRG018-2020SS.

References

Al-Kumaim, N. H., Alhazmi, A. K., Mohammed, F., Gazem, N. A., Shabbir, M. S. and Fazea, Y. 2021. Exploring the Impact of the COVID-19 Pandemic on University Students' Learning Life: An Integrated Conceptual Motivational Model for Sustainable and Healthy Online Learning. *Sustainability*, 13(5), p. 2546. Online Available from: http://dx.doi.org/10.3390/su13052546.

Aristovnik, A., Keržič, D., Ravšelj, D., Tomaževič, N. and Umek, L. 2020. Impacts of the COVID-19 Pandemic on Life of Higher Education Students: A Global Perspective. *Sustainability*, 12(20), p. 8438.

Blackmore, J. 2020. The Carelessness of Entrepreneurial Universities in a World Risk Society: A Feminist Reflection on the Impact of COVID-19 in Australia. *Higher Education Research & Development*, 39(7), pp. 1332–1336.

Demuyakor, J. 2020. Coronavirus (COVID-19) and Online Learning in Higher Institutions of Education: A Survey of the Perceptions of Ghanaian International Students in China. *Online Journal of Communication and Media Technologies*, 10(3), p. e202018.

Firang, D. 2020. The Impact of COVID-19 Pandemic on International Students in Canada. *International Social Work*, 63(6), pp. 820–824.

Gallagher, H. L., Doherty, A. Z. and Obonyo, M. 2020. International Student Experiences in Queensland during COVID-19. *International Social Work*, 63(6), pp. 815–819.

Martel, M. 2020. COVID-19 Effects on US Higher Education Campuses. *From Emergency Response to Planning for Future Student Mobility*. Institute of International Education, New York.

Misirlis, N., Zwaan, M., Sotiriou, A. and Weber, D. 2020. International Students' Loneliness, Depression and Stress Levels in COVID-19 Crisis: The Role of Social Media and the Host University. *Journal of Contemporary Education Theory & Research (JCETR)*, 4(2), pp. 20–25.

Mok, K. H., Xiong, W., Ke, G. and Cheung, J. O. W. 2021. Impact of COVID-19 Pandemic on International Higher Education and Student Mobility: Student Perspectives from Mainland China and Hong Kong. *International Journal of Educational Research*, 105, p. 101718.

Morgan, D. 1996. Focus Groups. *Annual Review of Sociology*, 22(1), pp. 129–152.

Morris, A., Hastings, C., Mitchell, E., Ramia, G., Wilson, S. and Overgaard, C. 2020. *The Experience of International Students before and during COVID-19: Housing, Work, Study and Wellbeing*. Sydney: University of Technology Sydney.

Nasir, M. I. M., Ramli, M. W. and Som, S. H. M. 2021. Now Look What You've Done, COVID-19! The Impact on Academic Survival among Postgraduate Students in Malaysia. *International Journal of Academic Research in Business and Social Sciences*, 11(2), pp. 604–618.

Novikov, P. 2020. Impact of COVID-19 Emergency Transition to On-line Learning onto the International Students' Perceptions of Educational Process at Russian University. *Journal of Social Studies Education Research*, 11(3), pp. 270–302.

Nguyen, O. O. T. K. and Balakrishnan, V. D. 2020. International Students in Australia – during and after COVID-19. *Higher Education Research & Development*, 39(7), 1372–1376

Peters, M. A., Wang, H., Ogunniran, M. O., Huang, Y., Green, B., Chunga, J. O., Quainoo, E. A., Ren, Z., Hollings, S., Mou, C. and Khomera, S. W. 2020. China's Internationalized Higher Education during COVID-19: Collective Student Autoethnography. *Postdigital Science and Education*, 2, pp. 968–988.

Sahu, P., 2020. Closure of Universities due to Coronavirus Disease 2019 (COVID-19): Impact on Education and Mental Health of Students and Academic Staff. *Cureus*, 12(4), p. e7541.

Schulmann, P., 2020. *Perfect Storm: The impact of the Coronavirus Crisis on International Student Mobility to the United States*. New York: World Education Services. Online Available from: https://wenr.wes.org/2020/05/

perfect-storm-the-impact-of-the-coronaviruscrisis-on-international-student-mobility-to-the-united-states.

Selvanathan, M., Hussin, N. A. M. and Azazi, N. A. N. 2020 Students Learning Experiences during COVID-19: Work from Home Period in Malaysian Higher Learning Institutions. *Teaching Public Administration*. doi: 10.1177/0144739420977900.

Sundarasen, S., Chinna, K., Kamaludin, K., Nurunnabi, M., Baloch, G. M., Khoshaim, H. B., Hossain, S. F. A. and Sukayt, A. 2020. Psychological Impact of COVID-19 and Lockdown among University Students in Malaysia: Implications and Policy Recommendations. *International Journal of Environmental Research and Public Health*, 17(17), p. 6206.

Wan Mohd Yunus W. M. A., Badri S. K. Z., Panatik S. A. and Mukhtar F. 2021. The Unprecedented Movement Control Order (Lockdown) and Factors Associated with the Negative Emotional Symptoms, Happiness, and Work-Life Balance of Malaysian University Students during the Coronavirus Disease (COVID-19) Pandemic. *Frontiers in Psychiatry*, 11, p. 566221. doi: 10.3389/fpsyt.2020.566221.

Yassin, A. A., Razak, N. A., Saeed, M. A., Al-Maliki, M. A. A. and Al-Habies, F. A. 2021. Psychological Impact of the COVID-19 Pandemic on Local and International Students in Malaysian Universities. *Asian Education and Development Studies*. https://doi.org/10.1108/AEDS-05-2020-0098

2 University students' online learning experience in Capstone unit

Liap-Teck Ong

2.1 Introduction

The COVID-19 pandemic has disrupted numerous industries all around the world. This includes the higher education sector. This study focuses on a Capstone practicum unit to gain insights into how this shift in delivery mode has affected the students' learning experience. Capstone units allow students to work on real-world issues in the industry under the guidance of academics with industry experience and experts in the industry. The findings of this study would facilitate the design and creation of better teaching and learning strategies for Capstone units. Capstone unit mimics real-life industry scenarios and provides opportunity for students to resolve real-world issues under the guidance of academics with industry experience with the help of subject matter experts from the industry.

2.2 Literature review

A review of the existing research and the debates on COVID-19's impact on higher education delivered online led to the emergence of three main discussion domains. The three domains are physical interactions, infrastructural support, and academic syllabus.

2.2.1 Physical interaction

One of the key differences between face-to-face and online learning is the absence of physical interaction between the students, their peers, and the academic staff. Since the start of the COVID-19 pandemic, several studies have been carried out to assess how this change impacts student learning (Adnan and Anwar, 2020; Lasfeto, 2020; Jung, Horta, and Postiglione, 2021; Neuwirth, Jović, and Mukherji, 2020). Lasfeto

DOI: 10.4324/9781003182733-3

(2020) found that social interaction is an important component of both face-to-face and online learning. However, the authors pointed out that this absence is felt more keenly during the COVID-19 pandemic as physical interactions are discouraged or not allowed outside the classroom. This is very different from the usual online learning setting where students could still have physical interactions with others beyond their cyber classrooms. A subsequent study by Baber (2021) reinforces the negative impacts the lack of physical interaction has on online learning. Baber (2021) found that the lack of social interaction is challenging for students in institutions of higher education as physical interactions has always been an important part of the learning process. However, Baber (2021) also reported that the students understand the need for social distancing measures and are able to take it in their stride. Jung *et al.*, (2021) further highlighted that "part of the learning experience in the campus environment is derived from communication in a natural environment" (Jung *et al.*, 2021, p. 6), an indication that their respondents consider online interactions less than natural. Similar findings were also obtained from the report by Curtin (2020) based on student feedback on online delivery.

Collectively, the studies above suggest the importance of physical interaction in the students' learning experience as it facilitates organic conversations and discussions, fellowship and friendship as well as a sense of camaraderie. The literature reveals that the lack of physical interaction brought about by the restrictions due to the COVID-19 pandemic is the one of the key challenges that needs to be addressed.

2.2.2 Infrastructural support

Infrastructural support for online learning is a key area to address (Crawford, *et al.*, 2020; Saxena, Baber and Kumar, 2020). Saxena *et al.* (2020) found that assurance, reliability, responsiveness, and website content are a few important factors affecting the students' learning experience. Furthermore, the study by Neuwirth *et al.* (2020) pointed out that the emotional, mental, financial, and pragmatic challenges faced by students could potentially be mitigated by infrastructural support in the form of a more human or passionate approach to student engagement. Maqsood *et al.*, (2021) go on to suggest that the providence of counselling and infrastructure for mental health could help alleviate any negative impacts faced by students. According to the study by Crawford et al. (2020) who examined the measures taken by universities from 20 countries to cope with the COVID-19 pandemic, the measures taken by these institutions are often moderated by financial and sustainability considerations. The study by Neuwirth *et al.* (2020) found that many institutions of higher education have set up technology support teams to support their academic staff and students who are less proficient in the technical aspects of online learning. The literature review reveals that infrastructural support both in technology and mental health is crucial for the successful transition to online learning during the COVID-19 pandemic.

2.2.3 Syllabus and assessment

Syllabus and assessment suitability to online learning is another area that impacts the students' learning experience (Rolim and Isaias, 2019; Shraim, 2019). Grading of online learning seems to affect the students' learning experience based on their perceptions on whether their assignments are graded objectively, fairly, and appropriately. A study by Shraim (2019) suggests that online assessments such as online exams are deemed more dependable, cost-effective, and efficient than traditional assessments by students. This finding supports the findings of Rolim and Isaias (2019) that students in higher education find e-assessments more practical, pragmatic, motivating, appealing, and enthralling than traditional assessments. The study by Petroski and Rogers (2020) examining the learning experience of students enrolled in a tertiary education institution in the USA, suggests that prior gameful learning experiences can help students to cope with sudden change in delivery. Their study is supported by a report by Curtin (2020) which suggests that prior online learning experiences, however limited, may help students adapt to fully online learning. The review of the literature suggests that online learning requires the customization of syllabus and assessments on an urgent basis.

2.2.4 Capstone units

In the business program for the host university, the completion of the Capstone unit is mandatory for all undergraduates. Typically, Capstone students are required to apply discipline knowledge and skills in real-life projects. Before the onset of the COVID-19 pandemic, the key feature of the Capstone unit is how it mimics real-life industry scenarios through face-to-face physical interactions between the lecturers, the students, and the industry partners. The students must resolve real-world issues under the guidance of academics with industry experience with the help of subject matter experts from the industry (Bartholomew, Newman and Newman, 2021; Boyas and Banerjee, 2021). However, the literature review suggests that the replacement of physical interaction in the Capstone unit is under-researched. The few studies on the online delivery of Capstone units include those by Gill and Mullarkey (2015) on information system management in Capstone units; Girard, Yerby, and Floyd (2016) on deep learning imbedded in Capstone units; Lee and Loton (2019) on purposes of Capstone units; and Blanford *et al.* (2019) on values of Capstone units.

This study differs from the aforementioned studies as (a) it focuses on a business unit; (b) it explores the students' learning experience; and (c) it focuses on the cohort of undergraduates who undertook the Capstone unit during the COVID-19 pandemic with no physical interactions and little preparations for the complete shift to online delivery. The learning experiences of students undertaking Capstone units under such circumstances need to be explored to provide necessary insights for the formulation of better learning and teaching strategies.

2.3 Research methodology

2.3.1 Research design

The dataset for the current study is based on the qualitative feedback from the survey, Student Feedback on Unit (SFU), conducted for all units at the end of each semester and completed by the students. The sample sizes are 24 from one semester and 51 from another semester, respectively, both semesters are from 2020. An interpretive analysis of the dataset is adopted for this study.

The students' qualitative feedback was subjected to cyclic readings and repeated interpretations to determine the main themes underpinning their learning experiences. This research approach is aligned with the interpretive research paradigm for lived experience research (Van Manen, 2016) and captures the experiences of the students.

2.3.2 Ethical consideration

Permission for the use of secondary data from the SFU was granted by the host institution and ethics clearance approved by the Human Research Ethics Committee (Ref: 20215406-5980).

2.3.3 Data collection

In the host institution, the SFU survey is conducted for all units at the end of each semester. Participation in the survey is voluntary, confidential, and anonymous. In the survey, students are asked to rate their experience and satisfaction with the units they have undertaken.

For consistency, the dataset is from the SFU results of the same Capstone practicum unit taught by the same lecturer.

2.4 Findings and discussion

2.4.1 Data Analysis

Through cyclic readings and repeated interpretations of the qualitative narratives, eight types of learning experiences were discerned. These eight types of experiences were further condensed into two main themes that best describe the students' learning experience, namely, accordance and discordance as depicted in Figure 2.1.

In the interpretive research paradigm on lived experience (Van Manen, 2016), the analysis is based on the condensation and conceptualization of the narratives of the participants' lived experiences in learning. Data analysis is carried out concurrently with data collection and the findings are perused and examined until the emergence of themes that best reflect the students' learning experience. Accordance is the first of two main themes. It signifies a learning experience that is agreeable, congruent, consonant, and meets the expectation of the students. On the opposite end of the spectrum, unfamiliarity with online learning and the lack of preparation led to discord in the learning process, hence the second main theme of discordance.

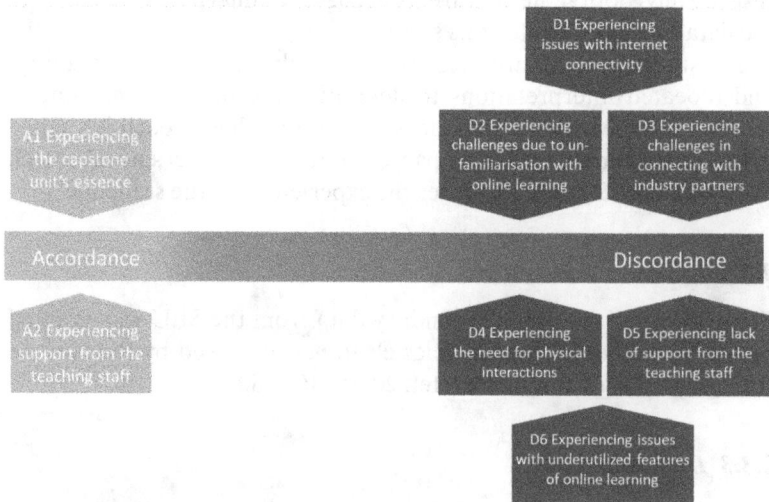

Figure 2.1 Eight types of learning experiences under two themes – accordance and discordance.

2.4.1.1 Accordance

A sense of accordance could be gleaned from the thematical analysis of the students' narratives pertaining to online learning for the participants. They could still appreciate the unique nature of the unit and benefit from their experiences. Some students also felt supported during their learning journey and had no issues connecting with their team as seen in the following sections.

2.4.1.1.1 EXPERIENCING THE CAPSTONE UNIT'S ESSENCE

The Capstone practicum unit is unique as it allows students to use their skills and knowledge to address real-world issues for which they are held accountable by a third party, their industry partners. Even though the unit was conducted online, the following narratives from the students' feedback suggest that they could still experience and appreciate the value offered by the practicum unit:

> *"The best aspect of this unit is to utilize our skills and knowledge and apply into actual industry work. This will give the students an experience on what does the industry expects"*

> *"Able to experience working as a team to solve real-live projects problems."*

> *"Being able to be exposed to real life experiences which are helpful for future careers while having online classes."*

> *"Having the opportunity to play the role as a member of a consulting team to provide advice and recommendations to representatives of a real-life company as a means of countering their inabilities as well as to develop the company's brand awareness among the targeted customers which I found to be a valuable experience for my future career because I was able to identify such issues that companies would face in the industry and discover various tactics not only from my team, but more was learned from the other teams involved with the unit."*

2.4.1.1.2 EXPERIENCING SUPPORT FROM THE TEACHING STAFF

Academic support for the Capstone practicum unit comes in the form of facilitating the interactions between the students and the industry partners, managing expectations on both sides and giving practical advice to help steer students in the right direction. The feedback from the students suggests that having good support allows them to enjoy the learning process.

> "So far everything is fine. Lecturer can still conduct online classes well and he is helpful and approachable when we face any difficulties in our studies."

> "The efforts of lecturer trying to give us the best explanation delivered online"

> 'The lectures were well-organized and clearly presented. I think every aspect of this class helped contribute to my learning experience."

> "The unit is very hands-on and varied quite a bit from the usual theory-heavy units that I was used to. I felt like I got to experience a different kind of learning and learnt a lot."

> "the information of what the students need to do as the week progress is great to let us prepare for the meeting"

> "We shared the ideas and opinions together during the online lecture and tutorial class. Even though we cannot have our class physically, we still open our webcam and have a face to face discussion."

> "I still get to work with people from different backgrounds, despite [the fact that] we had to do it virtually. I had fun planning the project although it can be overwhelming sometimes."

2.4.1.2 Discordance

Even in the traditional delivery mode, there will be students who express discordance with their learning experience. However, the shift to online delivery seems to have increased the levels of discordance experienced. This is perhaps a result of the challenges unique to online delivery as well as the abruptness of the shift. This theme is conceptualised based on the following experiences.

2.4.1.2.1 EXPERIENCING ISSUES WITH INTERNET CONNECTIVITY

The feedback from both cohorts suggests that the struggles with the technical aspect of online learning stemmed primarily from poor internet connectivity. This seems to be a common theme in other studies (Abbasi *et al.,* 2020; Adedoyin and Soykan, 2020; Osman, 2020). The relevant narratives are attached as:

> *"Do consider changing live presentation to pre-recorded presentation to avoid internet line disruptions. I have experienced a lot [of] internet disruption for the past 2 weeks and sometimes it causes inconvenience to my lecturer and fellow team mates."*

> *"some minor technical problem happened during the online meeting with our lecturer"*

> *"Lots of students are camera shy, awkward and silent doing video conferencing"*

> *"maybe the presentation with the clients can be done face to face because me personally have problems with internet connection"*

> *"the online deliveries may not effective sometimes"*

2.4.1.2.2 EXPERIENCING CHALLENGES DUE TO
UN-FAMILIARIZATION WITH ONLINE LEARNING

Although most courses and units in the host institution have some online components, a large chunk of learning and teaching still took place in person in classrooms. The sudden shift to online learning caused some issues for students less familiar with online delivery. This can be discerned from their narratives as quoted:

> *"just couldn't get use of online learning"*

> *"The absence of live lectures proves challenging for students to group assignments and presentations concurrently at uni."*

> *"It may be quite confusing and overwhelming by the announcement on canvas but it's manageable with the help of group members"*

> *"online learning in this was sooooo difficult (please go back to f2f after the pandemic ASAP"*

2.4.1.2.3 EXPERIENCING CHALLENGES IN CONNECTING
WITH INDUSTRY PARTNERS

One key feature of the Capstone unit is that the students could interact directly with their industry partners to understand their issues and their requirements before working together to come up with solutions to the problems presented. The shift to online learning caused some challenges in the students' communication with their industry partners. The relevant narratives are attached:

> *"Less information from client, many things based on assumption"*

> *"Without any communications with the industry partner, it would be difficult for me to grasp the objectives and requirements they need for me and my group to conduct research on."*

> *"the aspects that could be improve in this unit is probably more time spent with the client to able the students to gather more information"*

> *"During the meeting with the industry, I think there should be an assurance that the industry would reply to the question of the students."*

2.4.1.2.4 EXPERIENCING THE NEED FOR PHYSICAL INTERACTIONS

With the switch to online learning, all group work and discussions had to be done entirely online among students from different disciplines who previously had little to no interaction with one another. This could be the reason why some students in this study expressed the need for face-to-face interactions for group work and discussions. Relevant narratives from their narratives are attached as follows:

> *"The absence of live lectures proves challenging for students in group assignments and presentations concurrently at uni."*

> *"it's better if the class is made face to face as we need to discuss with our team member"*

2.4.1.2.5 EXPERIENCING A LACK OF SUPPORT
        FROM THE TEACHING STAFF

Online teaching differs from traditional face-to-face delivery and often requires a different set of pedagogical skills and techniques. While there was an adjustment period of 2 weeks in the first semester of 2020 before the shift to fully online learning, teething problems were still encountered by the students which likely affected their learning experience. An example of this issue is attached as follows:

> *"Online study is not good. [The] effectiveness to solve problems and have discussion is low."*

2.4.1.2.6 EXPERIENCING ISSUES WITH UNDERUTILIZED
        FEATURES OF ONLINE LEARNING

For the host institution, like most institutions of higher learning, there were already plans and steps taken to implement blended delivery or fully online courses before the pandemic. However, even with some infrastructure available to support the shift to online learning, the feedback from the students highlighted areas that could be further improved. The relevant narratives are as attached:

"Possibly the need for a topic on video conferencing".

"Post the recorded live meeting for students".

"Replay videos must be available".

2.5 Discussion

Two main themes emerged from the analysis of the students' learning experiences, namely accordance and discordance.

2.5.1 *Addressing accordance*

Accordance is derived from the positive experience of the students undertaking their Capstone unit online. Firstly, the study found that the students can still experience the unique essence of the Capstone unit through online study. Even online, they could experience working in a real business context. Given that the business environment has begun migrating towards online dialogues, meetings, conferences, and negotiations, the online nature of the Capstone unit could help prepare the students to work with business partners and carry out business transactions on online platforms.

The accordance experienced by the participants suggests a degree of adaptability and resilience among the students. A study by Martin *et al.* (2013) found that students who are adaptive have a competitive edge over their peers. These findings are similar to those of other studies (Abbasi *et al.*, 2020; Khalil et al., 2020). The positive experiences of the students indicate they could adapt quickly to unexpected changes and thrive.

Secondly, the support from the academic staff that have had considerable industry experience contributed to the positive experience of the students. Therefore, even in an online environment, the students could still experience, appreciate, and benefit from the support and guidance of the unit lecturer.

2.5.2 Addressing discordance

Although the Capstone unit has always been conducted face-to-face with no plans for online delivery, the positive findings from this study suggest that it can be successfully conducted online. This is an important finding for the faculty as it continues to evolve and improve to provide students with the best quality business education.

However, the study also discovered that the participants also encountered challenges and discordance. The sources of discordance are poor internet connectivity, un-familiarization with online learning, issues connecting with industry partners, the need of physical interactions, insufficient support from teaching staff, and the inadequacy of the infrastructural support.

The issue of poor internet connection adversely affecting the online learning experience in higher education is not unique. Several studies have come to the same conclusion: Abbasi *et al.*, (2020); Bryson and Andres (2020); Neuwirth *et al.*, (2020). Additionally, having a stable internet connection is vital as the students have to conduct extensive research and carry out online surveys on the computer. Some of the online final presentations also encountered challenges as some of the material for presentation encountered lagging due to inadequacies in the internet connection and WiFi services. While the speed of internet connection is usually not within the control of the academics, an empathic approach may help to mitigate the negative impact of poor internet connection.

The next finding from this study is that some of the students struggled with online learning due to un-familiarization with the delivery mode. Although other studies have found that millennials generally responded better to online learning, this study shows that some still struggled with the shift to online learning. Part of the struggle could be due to the suddenness of the shift. This highlights the need for special orientation programs and clear instructions to allow students to seamlessly transition from in-person studies to online learning.

The industry partner plays an integral role in the Capstone unit. With the shift to online learning, the study found a lack of readiness among the industry partners to connect and interact with the students online. As all interactions were conducted through email and video conferencing, the interactions were more stilted and constrained. A possible remedy for this issue is to have an orientation program for the industry partners to acclimatise them to academic requirements.

The lack of physical interaction also seems to affect the students' learning experience in the Capstone unit. Baber (2021) and Jung *et al.* (2021) postulated that learning is essentially a social activity and active engagement in these interactions has a substantial impact on the students' learning experience. This is one of the key weaknesses of online learning (Baber, 2021; Jung et al., 2021). The COVID-19 pandemic and its associated restrictions meant the complete absence of physical interaction among the students in the host institution. While the study shows their longing for physical interactions, particularly for this Capstone unit, there seems to be an acceptance of the situation as they understand the reason behind the restrictions.

Moreover, some students also report experiencing a lack of support from the teaching staff. In the host institution, there were no plans for the Capstone unit to be delivered online. The sudden shift meant that the teaching staff had to switch at a moment's notice with no precedence and no earlier planning as a guide. The solution is to provide relevant training and mentoring sessions to the academics by a team of academics experienced in online delivery and experts from the IT department.

Finally, the students also expressed a need for better infrastructural support for online learning. Before the pandemic, the host institution had been in the process of implementing blended and fully online delivery. This probably mitigated some of the impacts of the shift to online learning. However, most strategies for the shift to online delivery are gradual with constant refinement along the way. This scenario has been discussed in several other studies (Adnan and Anwar, 2020; Alqurashi, 2019; Altınay, 2017; Bryson and Andres, 2020; Curtin, 2020). The study supports the call for immediate improvements in infrastructural support in higher education.

2.6. Conclusion

In examining the students' qualitative feedback on the Capstone practicum unit during the COVID-19 Pandemic, this study discovered two main themes, accordance and discordance, underlying the students' learning experience. A sense of accordance comes from experiencing the essence and usefulness of the Capstone unit even through online delivery as well as the support and guidance of the academic staff. These findings suggest that while Capstone units have always been conducted face-to-face, they could be taught online without sacrificing their unique ability of allowing students to apply business principles and knowledge to real-world contexts. As the world is increasingly moving towards online transactions and virtual communications, the online learning of the Capstone unit may help prepare the students for working in a virtual business environment.

On the other hand, the students also encountered adverse learning experiences under the theme of discordance. A sense of discordance arises from issues with internet connection, challenges due to unfamiliarization with online learning, difficulties in dealing with industry partners, the need for physical interaction, the lack of support from teaching staff, and issues with online protocols and netiquette. With such insights, the author has identified a few key areas to improve the students' learning experience during online learning specifically applicable to Capstone business units. This includes (1) an empathic approach in student engagement, (2) the introduction of a special orientation program for the industry partners, (3) the creation of more active online discussion forums, and (4) special mentoring program for academics and students struggling with online delivery. Further studies are recommended to assess the effectiveness of the strategies derived from the study's findings.

Post-COVID realities and possibilities

This study suggests that an empathic teaching and learning approach, industry partner acclimatization, active online interactions, and timely counselling for academics and students are required to ensure the attainment of the learning objectives and outcomes of Capstone units delivered online. Post-COVID-19, such findings would still be relevant due to the trend towards online delivery in higher education. Accordingly, the insights into the learning and teaching of Capstone units during the COVID-19 pandemic provide important perspectives that facilitate the online delivery of Capstone units in the new normal.

References

Abbasi, S., Ayoob, T., Malik, A. and Memon, S. I. (2020). Perceptions of students regarding E-learning during COVID-19 at a private medical college. *Pakistan Journal of Medical Sciences*, 36(COVID19-S4), pp. S57–S61.

Adedoyin, O. B. and Soykan, E. (2020). COVID-19 pandemic and online learning: The challenges and opportunities. *Interactive Learning Environments*, pp. 1–13.

Adnan, M. and Anwar, K. (2020). Online learning amid the COVID-19 pandemic: Students perspectives. *Journal of Pedagogical Research*, 2(1), pp. 45–51.

Alqurashi, E. (2019). Predicting student satisfaction and perceived learning within online learning environments. *Distance Education*, 40(1), pp. 133–148.

Altınay, Z. (2017). Evaluating peer learning and assessment in online collaborative learning environments. *Behaviour & Information Technology*, 36(3), pp. 312–320.

Baber, H. (2021). Social interaction and effectiveness of the online learning – A moderating role of maintaining social distance during the pandemic COVID-19. *Asian Education and Development Studies*.

Bartholomew, D. E., Newman, C. M. and Newman, L. M. (2021). A snapshot of the marketing Capstone course at U.S.-based AACSB schools. *Marketing Education Review*, 31(1), pp. 26–40.

Blanford, J., Kennelly, P., King, B., Miller, D. and Bracken, T. (2019). Merits of Capstone projects in an online graduate program for working professionals. *Journal of Geography in Higher Education*, 44(1), pp. 45–69.

Boyas, E. and Banerjee, H. (2021). Integrative Capstone Assignment in Core MBA Curriculum. *Developments in Business Simulation and Experiential Learning: Volume 48*, pp. 108–125.

Bryson, J. R. and Andres, L. (2020). COVID-19 and rapid adoption and improvisation of online teaching: Curating resources for extensive versus intensive online learning experiences. *Journal of Geography in Higher Education*, 44(4), pp. 608–623.

Crawford, J., Butler-Henderson, K., Rudolph, J., Malkawi, B., Glowatz, M., Burton, R., Magni, P. and Lam, S. (2020). COVID-19: 20 countries' higher education intra-period digital pedagogy responses. *Journal of Applied Learning & Teaching*, 3(1), pp. 1–20.

Curtin, E. (2020). *UCC Students' Union Student Feedback on Online Learning Report (Ver5) Dec 2020*. Cork, Ireland: University College Cork.

Gill, T. G. and Mullarkey, M. T. (2015). Taking a case method capstone course online: A comparative case study. *Journal of Information Technology Education*, 14, pp. 189–218.

Girard, J. P., Yerby, J. and Floyd, K. (2016). Knowledge retention in Capstone experiences: An analysis of online and face-to-face courses. *Knowledge Management & E-Learning: An International Journal*, 8(4), pp. 528–539.

Jung, J., Horta, H. and Postiglione, G. A. (2021). Living in uncertainty: The COVID-19 pandemic and higher education in Hong Kong. *Studies in Higher Education*, 46(1), pp. 107–120.

Khalil, R., Mansour, A. E., Fadda, W. A., Almisnid, K., Aldamegh, M., Al-Nafeesah, A., Alkhalifah, A. and Al-Wutayd, O. (2020). The sudden transition to synchronized online learning during the COVID-19 pandemic in Saudi Arabia: A qualitative study exploring medical students' perspectives. *BMC Medical Education*, 20(1), p. 285.

Lasfeto, D. (2020). The relationship between self-directed learning and students' social interaction in online learning environment. *Journal of e-Learning and Knowledge Society*, 16(2), pp. 34–41.

Lee, N. and Loton, D. (2019). Capstone purposes across disciplines. *Studies in Higher Education*, 44(1), pp. 134–150.

Maqsood, A., Abbas, J., Rehman, G. and Mubeen, R. (2021). The paradigm shift for educational system continuance in the advent of COVID-19 pandemic: Mental health challenges and reflections. *Current Research in Behavioral Sciences*, 2, p. 100011. Available at: https://journals.sagepub.com/doi/pdf/10.1177/1477971420947738 [Accessed 24 March 2021].

Martin, A. J., Nejad, H. G., Colmar, S. and Liem, G. A. D. (2013). Adaptability: How students' responses to uncertainty and novelty predict their academic and non-academic outcomes. *Journal of Educational Psychology*, 105(3), 728–746.

Neuwirth, L. S., Jović, S. and Mukherji, B. R. (2020). Reimagining higher education during and post-COVID-19: Challenges and opportunities. *Journal of Adult and Continuing Education*, Available at: https://doi.org/10.1177/1477971420947738 [Accessed 24 December 2020].

Osman, M. E. (2020). Global impact of COVID-19 on education systems: The emergency remote teaching at Sultan Qaboos University. *Journal of Education for Teaching*, 46(4), pp. 463–471.

Petroski, D. J. and Rogers, D. (2020). An examination of student responses to a suddenly online learning environment: What we can learn from gameful instructional approaches. *Journal of Literacy & Technology*, 21(2), pp. 102–110.

Rolim, C. and Isaias, P. (2019). Examining the use of e-assessment in higher education: Teachers and students' viewpoints. *British Journal of Educational Technology*, 50(4), pp. 1785–1800.

Saxena, C., Baber, H. and Kumar, P. (2021). Examining the moderating effect of perceived benefits of maintaining social distance on e-learning quality during COVID-19 pandemic. *Journal of Educational Technology Systems*, 49(4), pp. 532–554.

Shraim, K. (2019). Online examination practices in higher education institutions: learners' perspectives. *Turkish Online Journal of Distance Education*, 20(4), pp. 185–196.

Van Manen, M. (2016). *Researching Lived Experience: Human Science for an Action Sensitive Pedagogy*. New York: Routledge.

3 Online assessments for university students

A case study of a business school

Devika Nadarajah

3.1 Introduction

3.1.1 Background

The COVID-19 pandemic is regarded as a global crisis jeopardising not only in numerous countries' public health systems but also their economic and societal well-being. Among the most adversely impacted sectors globally is the education sector, wherein teaching and learning have been massively disrupted at all levels. According to UNESCO (2020), more than 188 countries were forced to shut down their educational institutions, affecting 1.6 billion children, youth, and families. Giannini et al. (2020) reported that higher education institutions (HEIs) followed suit, shutting down campuses, and rapidly shifting to alternative teaching and learning platforms.

In an attempt to rapidly respond to the crisis, Gouëdard et al. (2020) proposed recommendations on education for OECD countries through the OECD (2020-1) education policy perspectives, albeit fully appreciating that a one-size-fits-all approach is not feasible. Nevertheless, the toolkit guided policy makers in devising realistic response strategies for their local contexts. Following these guidelines, the education landscape in Malaysia saw a swift change from traditional teaching and learning to online distance learning, through both synchronous instruction via online classrooms and asynchronous instruction via self-directed learning content, mindful of the need to maintain quality education. In fact, though cancelling all forms of teaching was an option, more than 90 percent of HEIs around the world shifted from traditional classroom learning to distance learning (IAU, 2020).

DOI: 10.4324/9781003182733-4

3.1.2 Problem statement

The shift to online teaching and learning naturally posed questions on the examination system. While there have been various endeavours towards the adoption of digital technologies in the classroom over the last decade, methods of administering examinations have remained traditional (Guàrdia et al., 2016). Nevertheless, the Ministry of Higher Education in Malaysia, in tandem with the Malaysian Qualification Agency (MQA), issued several directives for HEIs to transition to alternative methods to assess the achievement of student learning outcomes. This categorically left all HEIs with a relatively free hand to navigate unchartered waters. While some institutions were somewhat accustomed to online assessments, many that were rooted in conventional face-to-face examination systems found themselves facing the dilemma of developing assessments that meet distance learning requirements without compromising quality. Limited research has been carried out on institutions making a shift from conventional examinations to online assessments (Guàrdia et al., 2016; Ronnie, 2017; Yuk, 2019).

Therefore, this chapter closely examines a postgraduate business school in Malaysia which, after carefully examining various alternatives amid its ongoing trimester, made it compulsory for all students registered during the trimester to take online examinations in lieu of final face-to-face sit-in examinations. In particular, the school decided to replace face-to-face sit-in examinations with online examinations employing the case study analysis approach. Case study is an instructional method with reference to any scenario for the purpose of in-depth analysis and discussion. While problem-based learning using case studies have been part of the school's coursework assessments throughout trimesters, it was never implemented in final examinations. Moreover, though final examinations in the past have contained short cases or scenario-based questions, they never had long case studies. The decision to proceed with case study analysis for final assessments was made because it calls for higher-order thinking and prevents academic dishonesty among postgraduate students (Guàrdia et al., 2016). Since students were already exposed to case study methods throughout their coursework, it was deemed that this approach would not pose a big challenge for them during online final examinations.

3.1.3 Research question

This study was conducted to answer the following research question:

> Is there any significant difference between the results of students whose final assessment was an online case study and

the results of previous cohorts who sat for face-to-face final examinations?

It is hoped that the findings will shed light on effective ways to navigate final examinations that sustain the quality, equity, and efficacy of student learning outcome assessments. Given that the adoption of digital technologies facilitates a variety of options for student assessment, this study ultimately underscores a suitable approach for teaching, learning, and examinations in the "new normal" future.

3.1.4 The challenge for a Malaysian business school

This study examines a Malaysian business school's response towards transitioning from traditional face-to-face final examinations to online assessments using case study analysis. The school's postgraduate management programmes have been fully accredited by the MQA, while the business school itself has been awarded two international accreditations. The decision to move forward with final examinations instead of calling them off was made so as not to disadvantage student learning and progress. However, it was not easy to take the bold decision of shifting gears to online assessments using case studies, since the institution has been deeply ingrained in the tradition of face-to-face final examinations. The business school's academic and administrative teams had never considered such a practice to even be appropriate for any university championing quality excellence. Yet, the pandemic posed the challenge of maintaining quality excellence while moving into online final assessments.

Taking these concerns into account, it was decided that an online case study analysis would be a good fit to assess students' higher-order thinking, reflection, and problem-solving (Guàrdia et al., 2016; Yuk, 2019). This mode of examination would also be suited to measure students' achievement of course learning objectives while overcoming the need for proctoring, as case studies require more application of theory rather than theory alone. Academics modified all final examination papers to follow the new convention, following which the papers were meticulously moderated to ensure that the new assessment method would satisfy the evaluation of course learning outcomes. Final examination procedures and guidelines were subsequently refined and communicated to academics and students. Academics were required to set up an online meeting with their students to invigilate the examination, while students were made to turn on their cameras throughout the exam. At last, the final assessment week arrived and students completed the online final assessments. The examination unit compiled the answer scripts and handed them to the academics for grading. Once all courses' grading was complete, the results were approved by the university Senate and released to the students. Ultimately, the new final examination process was successfully implemented and concluded.

Despite its effective completion, a nagging concern about the online assessment was whether quality had been compromised. How could the business school ascertain with confidence, to itself, MQA, and international accreditation bodies, that the new approach and its ensuing procedures maintained quality? This question can be answered by comparing the results of the current cohort with previous cohorts. Therefore, this study examined if:

> H_1: *There is a significant difference between students' results in online assessments using case study analysis and students' results in face-to-face sit-in final examinations under the same course learning objectives.*

3.2 Literature review

3.2.1 An overview of higher education in Malaysia

Over the past century, the landscape of higher education in Malaysia has changed dramatically. Today, Malaysia has 20 public HEIs and more than 400 private HEIs (Ismail, 2020). Yuk (2019) enunciated that Malaysia has made great strides towards becoming a world-class higher education hub in its effort to transform from a production-based economy to a knowledge-based economy by 2020. The Private Higher Education Act in 1996 allowed private HEIs to operate and prosper in Malaysia, attracting students from India, Bangladesh, Pakistan, Africa, Middle East, and Eastern Europe. The higher education vision was further transcribed in the Malaysia Education Blueprint for Higher Education 2015–2025, with plans to attract more domestic and foreign students and reach a target population of 867,000 students by 2025 (Ministry of Higher Education, 2016). Currently, international students contribute RM15.6 billion to the Malaysian economy.

Malaysia's education quality is established and maintained stringently by the MQA. The Malaysian Qualification Framework (MQA, 2017) outlines MQA's roles and responsibilities as:

> *"MQA derives its powers from an Act of Parliament (Act 679) which gives it powers to implement the Malaysian Qualifications*

Framework, to accredit higher educational programmes and qualifications, to supervise and regulate the quality and standards of higher education providers, to establish and maintain the Malaysian Qualifications Register and to provide for related matters. Thus, it proposes, advises, guides, administers and regulates the higher education and training sectors with specific reference to quality assurance".

The MQA developed a comprehensive accreditation and regulatory framework that has contributed significantly to the high standards of quality in Malaysian education. This is in line with expectations that the higher education industry will expand in the next 20 years and continue to serve as an export industry that harnesses the nation's socioeconomic growth.

3.2.2 Postgraduate studies

A vast amount of scholarship exists with regards to students, teachers, learning, and assessments in the postgraduate context. Over the last two decades, the teaching and learning approaches of postgraduate programmes have transitioned from traditional methods to online learning, experiential learning, active learning, and simulation games or gamification. Underpinning most research in this area is Piaget's theory of active learning, the cognitive load theory, and the theory of mastery learning. One example is Fadol et al.'s (2018) study of management students at a business school in the Middle East. They found that students in online and flipped classrooms perform better than their counterparts in traditional classrooms. Their study corroborated Piaget's theory of active learning, which states that learning occurs when students act on and implement new concepts and ideas as opposed to playing a passive role in traditional learning. Specifically, active learning takes place when a lecturer, instead of lecturing, allows students to work on a task to help them understand a concept. Active learning, thus, improves student engagement and enhances their learning, retention, and performance in assessments. Geramian et al. (2012) further revealed that conscientiousness and openness to experience, two traits positively related to active learning, are significantly related to academic achievement among international postgraduate students in Universiti Teknologi Malaysia.

Ronnie (2017) conducted a study among postgraduate management students in a South African university to examine students' perception of challenges and learning opportunities in dyadic group work. The study brought to light the importance of collaboration and cooperation as key competencies necessary for individuals in the 21st century workplace. Closer to home, Seow et al.'s (2019) work on experiential learning pedagogy in a Singaporean university revealed that interdisciplinary learning pedagogy is critical in developing problem-solving and critical thinking skills that equip students for the workplace. The researchers suggested that future studies should develop appropriate rubrics to examine the achievement of learning outcomes associated with the experiential learning pedagogy. It is noteworthy to examine, in this context, the effectiveness of the change of assessment delivery.

The internationalisation of education is embodied in the interconnections between education institutions and the system in which they operate (Liu and Willis, 2021). In this system, knowledge and its circulation among lecturers and international students alike pave the way for economic contributions. Thus, with all students (international and local) "studying at home" throughout the COVID-19 pandemic, Liu and Willis (2021) argue that pedagogical practices based on norms and values are part of broader institutional demands. Ultimately, it is time to go back to the basics by focusing on pedagogy. Nevertheless, Oyedotun (2020) acknowledged that the transition to online pedagogy has exposed inequalities and challenges that are more apparent in today's educational landscape.

3.2.2.1 Online assessments

In this regard, Massive Open Online Courses (MOOCs) have been incorporated in face-to-face teaching as a new form of blended learning. The early years of MOOCs implementation were driven by the learning theory of Connectivism (2009–2012), comprising openness, diversity, autonomy, and connected people within a network of diverse technologies who can share and create knowledge. However, post-2012 saw a shift to MOOCs (2012–2016) towards on-campus teacher-centred lectures delivered on platforms, which placed greater emphasis on learning analytics and assessments (Wei et al., 2021). de Moura et al. (2021) examined how MOOCs can be better integrated into blended learning, indicating that students favourably perceive its functional value and quality in the learning process. The design of MOOCs includes a host of activities and exercises which allow greater collaboration, interaction, instructional design, information, and support for students, thus transforming students into active learners. In line with this, Wei et al.'s (2021) systematic literature review of MOOCs in higher education revealed that a consideration of the assessment of learning outcomes at the beginning of course design could support the formulation of explicit assessment goals and, in this way, instruct learners to work towards learning outcomes. Moreover, the authors urge diversity in assessments for greater effectiveness.

Burden et al. (2019) addressed the concept of innovative mobile learning pedagogies and disruptive innovations among school-aged learners. The authors aptly pointed out that while mobile technologies and the like have become commonplace in daily life, the harsh reality is that pedagogies and schooling have not changed at such drastic levels, given the complexity of schools, the learning preferences of students, and the motivations of teachers. Burden et al. (2019) further stressed that there is a perennial tendency towards moral panic in mobile learning. In truth, new technologies support the promotion of 21st century skills and have a place in pedagogical transformations today. Taking it to the next level, Butler-Henderson and Crawford (2020) explained that the higher education sector is also part of the digitisation and automation wave that has affected all industries. However, though online learning, e-learning, and digital assessments are being rolled out across the globe, there is concern about the limited implementation of online invigilation. It is further argued that while there is plenty of scholarship surrounding online examinations, there is a dearth of discussion at the pedagogical and governance levels.

According to Vos (2015), assessment is a major research area in higher education. Assessments in higher education typically involve three themes: design, measurement, and validity of assessment instruments; evaluation and feedback on student performance; and development of alternative forms of assessment to develop the learner. Notably, authentic assessment is a popular alternative assessment as it better prepares students for the 21st century workplace in comparison to traditional assessments. For example, Vos (2015) conducted a study among educators to determine how student learning is assessed through authentic business-related simulations. Simulation games replicate real-world decision-making scenarios and require a higher level of decision-making competency among business students. Her study highlighted that most educators apply creative assessment practices following evidence-based principles. She further noted that scholarship has recently moved into examining the role of assessment in developing the learner. Taking her findings into consideration, Vos (2015) called for more evidence-based scholarly work on how lecturers can best prepare students for activities that fall under authentic assessment. Butler-Henderson and Crawford (2020) state that perception is the largest barrier to online examinations; however, once students have experienced online examinations, there is a preference for this format. Overall, the literature has reported that student performance does not significantly differ in final examinations across online and traditional modalities. This gives hope to us in Malaysia.

Apart from implementing teaching, learning, and assessment approaches that prepare students for the 21st century workplace, many business schools also pursue international accreditations. Beddewela et al. (2017) articulated that business schools in the UK are accredited by three main bodies, namely the Associate of Master of Business Administration (AMBA), the European Quality Improvement System (EQUIS), and the Association for the Advancement of Collegiate Schools (AACSB). Each of these accreditation bodies aims to regulate the quality of education in business schools. Likewise, in the Malaysian context, most business schools are accredited by either AMBA, AACSB, and/or EQUIS in addition to MQA. The notion is to establish world-class recognition, as envisioned by the Malaysian government. Hence, the mounting pressure exerted by the pandemic and the demand for high quality standards have driven business schools towards rapid innovation and digital transformation.

Accordingly, the shift from traditional face-to-face teaching to online teaching has gained a substantial level of acceptance and adoption in Malaysia. While HEIs practice a blend of the two approaches to varying degrees, the conventional approach to assessments has always been face-to-face sit-in final examinations. This is in line with the MQA's prescription of outcome-based evaluation (Biggs, 1996) and the constructive alignment of teaching, learning, and assessment to engender greater student engagement and performance. However, the COVID-19 pandemic pushed the need to re-think and re-engineer the concept of final examinations. Amidst the forced closure of HEIs, the MQA promptly issued circulars advising HEIs that they have the flexibility to design and implement the most appropriate final examination method as per their individual resource capabilities. In a nutshell, final examinations were allowed to take the form of alternative final assessments.

3.3 Method

The quantitative method using secondary data was employed to collect data and answer the research question. The sample data for this study comprised students' results in three postgraduate courses covering different domains and bodies of knowledge. The reason for narrowing down the data to only three courses was because only these three courses were taught by the same lecturer for both assessment formats – face-to-face sit-in final examination and online case study analysis. Therefore, while the group of students among the two cohorts varied, the lecturer who taught the course remained the same individual. This selection minimised potential bias between the two cohorts.

With consent from the university management and registrar, the examination results of the three courses were obtained from the examination unit of the university. The data included a total of 340 results records of all students who had registered for the courses and attended either a face-to-face sit-in final examination (prior to the COVID-19 pandemic; 147 results) or an online final assessment using case study analysis (during the COVID-19 pandemic; 193 results). The case study used for the online examination was of a similar format to the one employed during the formative assessment. An independent sample t-test was envisioned as the most appropriate statistical technique to test the hypothesis comparing both groups.

3.4 Findings and discussion

Analysis was performed on 340 student examination results for the three courses spanning two different cohorts for each course. Table 3.1 presents the demographic profile of the students.

Table 3.1 Demographic profile of postgraduate students on face-to-face and online assessments

Demographic characteristic	Face-to-face sit-in final examination cohort	Online final assessment using case study analysis cohort
Gender:		
Male	74	103
Female	73	90
Age:		
20–29 years of age	57	108
30–39 years of age	74	56
Above 40 years of age	16	29
Number of students per course		
Number of Students in Course 1	52	62
Number of Students in Course 2	44	61
Number of Students in Course 3	51	70
Total number of results (340)	**147**	**193**

Table 3.2 Descriptive statistics of examination results across three courses

Descriptive statistics	Course 1	Course 2	Course 3
Mean	76.53	72.93	74.74
Standard deviation	5.196	8.883	4.736
Skewness	0.148	−5.546	−1.764
Kurtosis	−0.166	3.840	4.420

There were 74 male students and 73 female students in the cohort who sat for face-to-face sit-in final examinations while 103 male students and 90 female students were involved in the online final assessment using case study analysis. Course 3 was observed to have the highest number of students across both student groups. With respect to age distribution, both cohorts recorded more students aged below 40 years old than older students. Overall, the profiles of both student cohorts were not substantially different from each other.

Next, Table 3.2 provides the descriptive statistics of the results of the three courses. All three courses had somewhat similar average results in the low- to mid-70s range, while Course 2 reported the highest standard deviation in results. According to Hair et al. (2018), skewness and kurtosis demonstrate the shape of a data's probability distribution, whereby a normal distribution should have skewness and kurtosis values within the range of ± 2. Only Course 1 appeared to be normally distributed, while Course 2 did not have acceptable skewness and kurtosis values and only skewness was within the acceptable range for Course 3. Upon examination of the q-q plot, however, it was observed that there were no significant departures from normality for Course 2 and Course 3.

Hypothesis testing was carried out using an independent sample t-test to compare the results of the two student cohorts for each course; that is, those who undertook a face-to-face sit-in final examination and those who undertook an online final assessment using case study analysis.

The results for Course 1 showed a mean difference of 1.23 with a t-statistic of −1.264 and a p-value of 0.209, which suggested rejection of the hypothesis at the 95 percent confidence level. For course 2, the mean difference was 3.43 with a t-statistic of −1.760 and a p-value of 0.084. Again, the hypothesis was rejected at the 95 percent confidence level. Finally, the hypothesis was also rejected at the 95 percent confidence level for Course 3, which had a mean of 1.06 with a t-statistic of 1.275 and p-value of 0.205. The analysis, thus, failed to observe any significant difference between the results of students who took a conventional face-to-face final examination and the results of students who took an online case study final assessment for Course 1, Course 2, and Course 3.

The results of the hypothesis testing, therefore, revealed that there were no substantial performance variations between students who had a traditional final examination experience and students who faced a sudden transition to the online platform for their final assessment using a case study analysis. The findings notably suggest that the overall quality of education in the business school remained intact despite the change of medium, thereby supporting and affirming the theory of mastery learning, outcome-based evaluation, and constructive alignment.

3.5 Conclusion

Viewed in a positive light, the COVID-19 pandemic has forced us to test the efficiency and flexibility of our education systems, acting as a wake-up call to remind us that even HEIs require a disaster recovery contingency plan. Beyond that, it has offered us the chance to openly explore and experiment with alternative approaches that bring stakeholders closer in the spirit of learning (OECD, 2020-1).

Having survived a year of the pandemic with online lessons and assessments, the time is ripe for HEIs to move towards resilience, quality, equity, and well-being in our education system (OECD, 2020-1). Resilience and quality ensure minimal disruptions to learning so that learning goals and competencies can be achieved by students; equity ascertains that students from the same cohort are not left behind; and well-being affirms that students' socio-emotional skills are not compromised. The outcome of this study is indeed aligned with these goals of the OECD.

Adapting student examinations to the online setting calls for HEIs to consider several parameters, such as the nature of courses, learning outcomes, and internal resource capacities. In this regard, the OECD (2020-2) has come forth with several alternatives to adapt on-site examinations to remote online settings: online proctoring, which is a solution to supervise remote examinations with the aim of reducing academic dishonesty; redesigning examinations by creating different models such as synchronous oral examinations; offering hybrid options that allow students to choose between proctored written examinations or oral examinations; varying sets of examination questions to minimise interactions among students; imposing stricter time limits for written examinations; and developing open-book written examinations with questions soliciting students' personal reflections or knowledge application that require deep critical thinking.

Therefore, while moving to remote online examinations is a suitable short-term measure, the suggestions offered by the OECD (2020-2) to adapt or adjust examinations should be applied in the long term. Oyedotun (2020) further offered suggestions to mitigate developing countries' challenges at the tertiary level, such as managing disparities in technology (i.e. internet access); providing technical assistance when required; transitioning gradually in situations where the home environment may not be conducive for learning; offering practical training sessions; and exploring phone modality for educational purposes. Butler-Henderson and Crawford (2020), on the other hand, recommended institutions to select systems that include biometrics with high precision, such as user authentication as well as movement, sound, and keystroke monitoring which report deviations. These features reduce the need for online examinations to be invigilated. Other system features could include system or browser locks and an interface design that makes the online examination more intuitive.

Efforts taken by institutions to improve the overall examination process during the COVID-19 crisis have eventually allowed greater reliability on online examinations and assessments leading towards the award of degrees. Such efforts do not only increase the credibility of degrees but also improve students' learning experiences and outcomes. In a statement at the World Economic Forum, Paul Kruchoski made two pertinent points – "*the university of tomorrow will also focus on 'learning to learn'*" and that "*the university of tomorrow is already here*" (Kruchoski, 2016). The Malaysian business school discussed in this chapter is indeed on track as a "university of tomorrow".

Post-COVID realities and possibilities

While the world is hopeful of a tomorrow without COVID-19, the education landscape has changed forever. The "new normal" of online teaching and assessments has paved the way for the continued adaptation of a hybrid approach. The post COVID-19 era will see teaching and learning implemented through a variety of learner-centric methods beyond the classroom setting. The same applies for assessments and examinations, which will include a combination of authentic and effective approaches that do not concede quality at any point.

References

Beddewela, E., Warin, C., Hesselden, F., & Coslet, A. (2017). Embedding responsible management education – Staff, student and institutional perspectives. *The International Journal of Management Education, 15*(2), 263–279.

Biggs, J. B. (1996). Enhancing teaching through constructive alignment. *Higher Education, 32*(3), 347–364.

Burden, K., Kearney, M., Schuck, S., & Hall, T. (2019). Investigating the use of innovative mobile pedagogies for school-aged students: A systematic literature review. *Computers & Education, 138*, 83–100.

Butler-Henderson, K., & Crawford, J. (2020). A systematic review of online examinations: A pedagogical innovation for scalable authentication and integrity. *Computers & Education, 159*, 104024.

de Moura, V.F., de Souza, A.C., & Viana, A.B.N. (2021). The use of Massive Open Online Courses (MOOCs) in blended learning courses and the functional value perceived by students. *Computers & Education, 161*, 104077.

Fadol, Y., Aldamen, H., & Saadullah, S. (2018). A comparative analysis of flipped, online and traditional teaching: A case of female Middle Eastern management students. *The International Journal of Management Education, 16*(2), 266–280.

Geramian, S. M., Mashayekhi, S., & Ninggal, M. T. (2012). The relationship between personality traits of international students and academic achievement. *Procedia – Social and Behavioral Sciences, 46*, 4374–4379.

Giannini, S., Jenkins, S., & J. Saavedra (2020). *Reopening schools: When, where and how?* UNESCO. https://en.unesco.org/news/reopening-schools-when-where-and-how

Gouëdard, P., Pont, B., & Viennet, R. (2020). *Education responses to COVID-19: Shaping an implementation strategy.* OECD Education Working Papers No. 224, OECD Publishing.

Guàrdia, L., Crisp, G., & Alsina, I. (2016). Trends and challenges of e-assessment to enhance student learning in higher education. In Cano, E., and Ion, G. (Eds.), *Innovative practices for higher education assessment and measurement* (pp. 233–389). IGI Global. Hershey, PA

Hair, J. F, Black, W.C, Babin, B.J., & Anderson, R.E. (2018). *Multivariate data analysis* (8th Ed.). Prentice Hall. DOI: 10.4018/978-1-5225-0531-0.ch003

IAU (2020). *The impact of COVID-19 on higher education around the world.* International Association of Universities. https://www.iau-aiu.net/IMG/pdf/iau_covid19_and_he_survey_report_final_may_2020.pdf

Ismail, A. F. (2020). *Facts, figures matter in MoE, MoHE rightsizing.* New Straits Times. https://www.nst.com.my/opinion/columnists/2020/01/558581/facts-figures-matter-moe-mohe-rightsizing

Kruchoski, P. (2016). *10 skills you need to thrive tomorrow—and the universities that will help you get them.* World Economic Forum. https://www.weforum.org/agenda/2016/08/10-skills-you-need-to-thrive-tomorrow-and-the-universities-that-will-help-you-get-them.

Liu, T. & Willis, K. (2021). Cut and paste pedagogy? Academic mobility, teaching practices and the circulation of knowledge. *Geoforum, 119*, 11–20.

Ministry of Higher Education (2016). *Malaysia education blueprint 2015–2025 (higher education)*. Ministry of Higher Education Malaysia. http://mohe.gov.my/muat-turun/awam/penerbitan/pppm-2015-2025-pt/5-malaysia-education-blueprint-2015-2025-higher-education

MQA. (2017). *Malaysian quality framework*. Malaysian Qualification Agency. https://www.mqa.gov.my/pv4/mqf.cfm

OECD. (2020-1). *Education responses to COVID-19: An implementation strategy toolkit*. OECD Education Policy Perspectives No. 5, OECD Publishing.

OECD. (2020-2). *Remote online exams in higher education during the COVID-19 crisis*. OECD Education Policy Perspectives No. 6, OECD Publishing.

Oyedotun, T. D. (2020). Sudden change of pedagogy in education driven by COVID-19: Perspectives and evaluation from a developing country. *Research in Globalization, 2*, 100029.

Ronnie, L. (2017). Dyadic processes in postgraduate education: Insights from MBA student experiences. *The International Journal of Management Education, 15*(3), 513–519.

Seow, P.S., Pan, G., & Koh, G. (2019). Examining an experiential learning approach to prepare students for the volatile, uncertain, complex and ambiguous (VUCA) work environment. *The International Journal of Management Education, 17*(1), 62–76.

UNESCO. (2020). *Global monitoring of school closures caused by COVID-19*. UNESCO. https://en.unesco.org/covid19/educationresponse

Vos, L. (2015), Simulation games in business and marketing education: How educators assess student learning from simulations. *The International Journal of Management Education, 13*(1), 57–74.

Wei, X., Saab, N., & Admiraal, W. (2021). Assessment of cognitive, behavioral, and affective learning outcomes in massive open online courses: A systematic literature review. *Computers & Education, 163*, 104097.

Yuk, F. C. (2019). Malaysia: From hub to exporter of higher education and implications. *International Journal of Business and Social Science, 10*(2), 48–54.

4 Video log (Vlog) for enhancing speaking skills in the ESL classroom

Thilaga Ravinthar
and Khursiah Mohd Sauffi

4.1. Introduction

The COVID-19 pandemic outbreak has caused many industries to seek alternative measures. The education sector was also forced to opt for online education due to closure of physical learning facilities. In Malaysia, higher learning institutions were advised to be online till 31st December 2020 and only certain students could be on campus with strict measures (NST, 2021). It is known that university students are exposed to online learning earlier in their lectures through their Learning Management System portal. Conducting the lessons online throughout the semester, however, poses various challenges to educators and students. Therefore, for English as a Second Language (ESL) students, the assessments had to be amended as a measure to fulfil student learning needs.

In teaching and learning a language, reading, listening, speaking, and writing skills are emphasised. Speaking is one of the crucial segments prioritised in language learning at university because of the importance of language proficiency for employability. Students may not have the opportunity to exercise English in daily communication and the COVID-19 outbreak has impacted real-time conversation as well (Syafri & Endrizal, 2020).

The outbreak of COVID-19 pandemic demanded an alternative approach in teaching communicative skills to students and speaking skill is believed to be one of the most challenging parts of teaching and learning. According to Mandasari and Aminatun (2020), students perceive Video log (Vlog) as a positive tool in assisting speaking skills in providing engagement and motivation. This idea is supported by Madzlan, Seng, and Kesevan (2020) as they assert that technology integration in the learning process results in positive engagement among students to use the target language (Madzlan et al., 2020).

Vlog commonly known as Video-Blogging is used as a communicative medium for information sharing (Masofa & Rahmah, 2018).

DOI: 10.4324/9781003182733-5

It allows students to record their presentation for upload on the Internet through some sharing sites such as *YouTube* and *Facebook*. Technology usage in the university aligns with the mission to transform the future of education to meet Industrial Revolution 4.0 challenges in staying relevant and competitive in new living settings.

The main objective of this research is to investigate Vlog as a speaking learning tool for ESL learners during the COVID-19 pandemic and to identify the challenges learners faced in completing their assignments. Much of English language teaching in conventional times has frowned upon the use of new technologies in the classes. The focus on speaking is a crucial one as most course activities have dealt with face-to face exercises in the classroom. The same applies to the instructor-learner classroom interaction. The COVID-19 pandemic pushed both educators and learners to use technologies as a core aspect of their work. It is commendable that the lockdown period encouraged students to spend more time online and gain technology knowledge and skills which assisted in the Vlog production process besides connecting themselves with the rest of their peers to complete this group project. Vlog has been actively used in English Language learning to assist with speaking anxiety among students and the present study aims at exploring Vlog usage during the COVID-19 pandemic as a learning instrument for speaking skills.

This study is guided by two research questions:

1   How do ESL students describe their experience of using Vlog to learn speaking?
2   What are the challenges faced by the students in completing the Vlog task?

4.2 Literature review

Speaking skill is one of the finest communication skills that need to be developed among undergraduates. However, due to the pandemic, students had no access to physical interaction and other communicative activities that could be conducted in face-to-face-lessons. The teaching and learning process adapted into virtual and the lessons were conducted remotely (Sanford, 2020).

Unlike other skills in language learning, the speaking skill needs to be assessed individually although the task is assigned as a group assignment. Each student will have to perform based on the speaking skill assessment rubric which aims at guiding students in preparing their Vlog. The assessment rubric for this task focused on content, pronunciation, vocabulary, and fluency which is in line with the speaking performance criteria. Malaysian students learn English for 11 years since primary school and students in higher learning institutes are expected to have adequate knowledge in using the language to express their thoughts (Eng, Saeed & Mohamed Ismail, 2019). In acquiring a Second Language (SLA), students are able to learn the target language with the aid of technology in an informal setting (Tarighat & Khodabakhsh, 2016).

4.2.1 *Vlog as an effective tool for speaking assessment*

Computer Mediated Communication (CMC) allows students to participate effectively using the target language without prejudice and this permits students to be creative in expressing themselves (Codreanu & Combe, 2019). Vlog usage encourages students to develop their speaking skills by focusing on vocabulary, fluency, pronunciation, and content. Production of Vlog requires students to master vocabulary as it is the centre of language communication. Researching on global issues and doing presentations provides them with the platform to acquire the most used words in ESL (Alkurtehe et al., 2019). A large number of university students acknowledged that Vlog improved their speaking skills (Thulasi Palpanadan et al., 2021). This concedes with the notion of Vlog as an alternative learning tool in teaching speaking skills due to positive responses from students (Anggraeni et al., 2020).

4.2.2 *Vlog as a feasible task for speaking assessment*

Students were encouraged to upload their Vlogs on platforms such as *YouTube* and *Facebook*. Such an activity is very popular among the students. Many students today are savvy users of technology and Vlogs are deemed as suitable learning assignments for virtual classrooms in the COVID-19 era. According to Maulidah (2018), there are certain stages in producing a Vlog and each stage has functions and certain processes for students to implement. The main stages of a Vlog include conceptualising, brainstorming, articulation, monitoring and evaluating and this framework was found to be useful for guiding students to work on their assignments in the present study.

4.3 Methodology

This study used a qualitative method to gather broad data about student experiences in completing Vlog for speaking activity in ESL classrooms during the COVID-19 pandemic. Students' responses after completing the task were elicited. Students' views on their experiences in completing the task, challenges faced and their suggestions for future consideration of instructors were elicited. The participants of this study were nine undergraduate students in a Malaysian public university who were taking an English language proficiency course and who led their teams in completing the Vlog. The students had to complete a speaking activity, using the guidelines offered by Maulidah (2018). The instructors had to supervise the students' work at every stage of the production process Attention was given to how the students used the different processes in steering their work.

4.3.1 Vlog instructions

The students were assigned to produce a 15-minute Vlog on current issues. The Vlog mirrored the discussion format and students were given autonomy to choose their own topic. In this speaking assignment, students were assessed mainly on (i) vocabulary, which required them to use accurate words to address the issue; (ii) fluency that is measured through their organisation of ideas; (iii) pronunciation focused on the correct articulation of words; and (iv) content that is appropriate as it reflects the goal of Vlog.

In the first stage, the instructors explained the task to the students and gave them the assignment guidelines. Samples of Vlog were shown and a question and answer session was conducted. After that, the students chose their own group members. In the second stage, the students were given two weeks to choose a topic for their Vlog. The students prepared a draft on the topic comprising the introduction, contents and conclusion. Then, they were required to brainstorm for their video script with the group members. Upon finalising the content, they were required to share the draft with the instructor to ensure continuous communication despite online learning being conducted throughout the semester. The instructor checked the draft and discussed necessary improvements with the students. The articulation stage would be the process of students working on their Vlog through practice and editing. Prior to submission, monitoring provided them the avenue for them for listening to and editing their video. In the last stage of evaluation, the submitted Vlog would be assessed based on the criteria of vocabulary, fluency, pronunciation, and content.

4.3.2 Data collection and data analysis

An interview protocol for undergraduates was designed to collect data for this study. Some 15 questions were constructed. The questions were divided into three parts. Part 1 focused on the demographic information. In Part II, the students were asked about their experience in preparing a Vlog for their speaking assessment and in Part III, the questions covered the challenges they faced in completing the task. A pilot test was conducted with a group of similar target participants using the interview protocol. The pilot test participants were undergraduates also in the same course but in a different semester. The questions were found to be relevant and comprehensible and helpful in revealing insights on students' voices.

In analysing the data, the interview transcripts were read to understand the overall responses provided by the students. The researcher then started coding data from interview transcripts into several suitable themes and descriptions. The major themes that emerged from the students' perspective include (i) The Use of Vlog as a Speaking Learning Tool, (ii) Challenges of the Task, and (iii) Suggestions for Improvements.

4.4 Findings and discussion

Findings from the interview were coded thematically to answer two research questions which were to examine the use of Vlog as a speaking tool and the challenges faced by learners in the ESL classrooms in completing the task during the COVID-19 pandemic. It revealed that Vlog could serve as a speaking task that engaged the students and instructors. Student engagement occurs due to the capability of technology in connecting students (Wulandari, 2019) as they become involved in different stages of the activity to ensure they upload good work.

The project revealed that clear instructions must be given, and instructors should demonstrate the steps and task objectives to ensure students are well prepared and informed on the expected task learning outcomes. The instructors can provide learning materials, tips, and guidebooks that will enhance student performance in language learning in the ESL classroom as noted by many scholars (Ajoke, 2017). This research also highlighted how alternative approaches to face-to-face classroom presentations can be used in teaching speaking skills. More crucially, we are facing new realities where students may not always be physically present to engage in real-time communication. The Vlog concept of teaching speaking skills for undergraduates was accepted positively and has revealed many benefits and this is in line with previous studies on technology usage in enhancing teaching of English among the younger generation by Wulandari (2019).

4.4.1 The use of Vlog as a learning tool

To answer Research Question 1 'How do ESL students describe their experience of using Vlog to learn speaking?', online interviews were conducted with study participants and the following views were unveiled.

4.4.1.1 Task feasibility

This task was considered feasible, as all the students confirmed that they managed to complete their Vlog to share experiences, thoughts and ideas on certain topics. The task was described as an economical and a time-saving task. Even though it was not easy to complete, the task was portrayed as an interesting activity that involved many new challenging skills and creativity by the participants.

> *"Yes I do. Vlog is designed to share experiences, thoughts, and ideas with audiences..."*
>
> *(Student 1)*

> *"Yes, me and my groupmates do a Vlog about the benefits of Tabata... You don't have to spend money at all, [you] can do [it] anywhere and anytime."*
>
> *(Student 7)*

> *"Yes, I did... It's actually quite interesting as I've seen some Vlogs but I never thought I would be doing one. Vlog is not as easy as it seems."*
>
> *(Student 2)*

4.4.1.2 Benefits of the task

All participants confirmed that they liked doing Vlog because they could speak and share ideas and knowledge without writing lengthy reports about their work. It could be assumed that these students prefer to do speaking rather than writing tasks:

> *"Yes, I enjoy this task. Vlogging allows me to share ideas and demonstrate knowledge without text. Not all are great writers and by allowing us to use a Vlog for a project can give me the ability to demonstrate what I know and confidence to do it in a way that I feel the most comfortable."*
>
> *(Student 1)*

Apart from that, this task improved their video production skills, speaking skills, and confidence levels in front of the camera. In fact, all of them admitted that this task improved their speaking skills as they felt confident speaking in English language. This was because they had the opportunity to practice speaking before recording their Vlog and make necessary improvements such as in terms of pronunciation and tone of voice prior to submission. The task elevated the fear in them yet assisted them to speak with less anxiety:

> *"Yes, I like doing this task because I can learn how to do [make a] Vlog. It also makes me learn how to edit videos, how to practice speaking, and also teaches me on what to put inside the video so it is simple, nice and informative."*
>
> *(Student 5)*

> *"Absolutely Yes! I like that task because it can help me to be more confident to talk about a topic."*
>
> *(Student 3)*

> *"I have a very soft voice and I also have nervousness while recording. So whenever I record myself talking, I can barely hear it. This assignment really improved my speaking skills and my confidence level."*
>
> *(Student 2)*

> *"Yes, because I think I only speak English in English class. So in this assignment it helped me to speak English better."*
>
> *(Student 5)*

Vlog was an advantage for some students who were familiar with it. Much to their excitement, several students found that they learnt a more systematic way of producing their work using the Maulidah (2018) guidelines. Therefore, this proved that using technologies for learning English, specifically in improving speaking skills, is important for students:

> *"Yes, I do like the task. This is because I am familiar with similar kinds of tasks... as I have done quite a lot of recorded speaking tasks, like Vlog, back in my diploma years. But now, we are able to organise the different stages properly so that we are able to upload our work and share with many viewers. We were also careful to make*

sure that we paid attention on vocabulary, pronunciation and the content of the topic."

(Student 6)

4.4.1.3 Choice of topics

All the participants liked that they were allowed to choose their own topics. Most of the topics chosen were under the themes of lifestyle, technology, nature and health and sports such as Vlog about Tabata, Healthy Lifestyle, Cyberbullying, Online Learning during COVID-19, Outdoor Recreation, Pollution, and Lee Chong Wei. The students chose their respective topic to explore it, so it was a way of learning and sharing information. Some of them wanted to create awareness about the topic:

"We in the team chose the topic ourselves and of course we liked it."

(Student 3)

"Yes, I like the choices of topics given. This is because students get to choose which topic that they want to discuss and present."

(Student 6)

"I love the topic as it is something related to my experience and my life ... I feel that it brings much joy to me ..., I love to share my passion with other people and share some information about outdoor recreation."

(Student 8)

"Our Vlog's topic was Cyber bullying... as it was one of the hot issues back then... We made this Vlog to create an awareness among us... And we learnt about ways to be careful when sharing pictures and texts in social media as it can be used for teasing and shaming users. We also learnt about learning to be respectful and treating our friends with kindness, even though we do not like their posts on the Internet."

(Student 2)

The students also preferred to choose common issues that they were confronting in a very difficult time. Most of the issues were related to the COVID-19 pandemic and current challenges faced by students in the country. It can be assumed that the students were able to express their ideas more fluently when given topics that were interesting and relevant as they could talk about it in a productive way in their activities:

> *"Cyberbullying... it was based on one of the current experiences faced by students who faced anxiety, sadness, anger and frustration when they interact with some of their online friends."*
>
> *(Student 2)*

> *"Drunk driving has received much attention in social media. There are many controversial views and users had different views about it. We decided to do the topic because as we know, many deaths happened in our country because of drunk drivers and we felt that we need to share some of the sorrow felt by victims."*
>
> *(Student 9)*

4.4.1.4 Working in a group

All the students sampled agreed that this task was better conducted in a group rather than individually because they were able to discuss ideas and divide tasks in order to manage their time wisely. Since the project required students to organise their work in a detailed way and some of them were facing technical difficulties, the students voted for the assignment in groups. The students also could evaluate each other's work before compilation and submission.

The pandemic posed different challenges to students who were working with different skills in their homes. Many restrictions were imposed and outdoor filming in groups was not advisable during the period. So, the students had to cooperate and manage their tasks so that they learn about teamwork. It appeared that they valued peer evaluations and sharing of ideas among them as they all wanted to be proud of the work being uploaded to the Internet. Some of the views on group work were as follows:

> *"Yes, because it helps us to plan accordingly and manage our time equally."*
>
> *(Student 2)*

> *"Yes, because there are a lot of opinions and ideas that we can hear. So, the result will become much better."*
>
> *(Student 4)*

"I think it is better done in groups as students can do peer evaluations among themselves while completing it."

(Student 6)

4.4.1.5 Time frame of the task

All the students claimed that seven weeks was enough for them and their group members to work on the Vlog. They had time to brainstorm for ideas, search for information on their topic, plan for content and storyline, and do the recording. Given that they had to work on different stages of the production and report to their instructors consistently, the time factor was an important one, specifically in this case where they were not used to production activities in their learning programmes. Some of the participants did not seem to worry about video editing; they even mentioned that they had enough time to record and edit their video properly before uploading their works:

"I think seven weeks was sufficient to complete the task because the duration for the video was quite short, thus making it easier to record... seven weeks are more than enough for us to find information regarding the topics."

(Student 6)

"Sufficient. Doing Vlog videos is actually pretty simple, since this is a group project so we can divide parts with each member... makes it easier, fun and interesting as we learn about speaking skills."

(Student 7)

"I think seven weeks is an appropriate time to complete the task for me, I have enough time to do brainstorming, script planning, filming practices, editing and sound mixing ... The activity involved many technical skills that were new to us and we had to learn new things every week... and from home. Also, we had to give attention to the information and language in our work."

(Student 8)

4.4.1.6 Instructions

All of the students concurred that the given instructions on the assignments were clear as they were told about the duration, content to highlight and aspects to avoid. Other than that, a weekly Question and Answer session was conducted about the task. The use of Google Docs in drafting the storyboard also helped the students in completing the task as they could always interact with the lecturer via Google Docs:

"Yes, the instructions for the task given were clear. This is because the instructions were given in detail, like the duration of the video and certain details that the lecturer wanted students to highlight in their Vlog."

(Student 6)

"The lecturer will open the Q&A session for us, and also give us a lot of tips on how to do the different stages of the task. We found the stage of articulation quite challenging and the instructions and views of the lecturer were important. We had to practise many times and make sure that the content-creation included images, graphics and other visuals that was interesting. The instructions from the lecturer in recording the video was also useful and we had to learn many things independently."

(Student 7)

"The lecturer kept explaining until all of us got the idea. Besides, she used Google Docs for us to write our ideas and comment on them. So, we know which part to improve... based on the feedback. I think the lecturer's role is important in completing the assignment as making a video, compared to speaking in front of the class is very different."

(Student 4)

Besides that, the majority of the students agreed that it was better that samples of Vlog were provided in order to get some ideas on how to start doing the task. Samples also helped them to understand better about the task as some of them had never done a Vlog before. Some student participants, however, thought that they did not need to be provided with samples of Vlog, as they believed that they should try to do the task on their own. Further, they also believed that it would cause more pressure if they had to refer to samples and it would lessen their creativity. The different views of the students can be seen below:

"It is much better when samples are provided. Maybe some of us don't know what is a Vlog ... this is a new activity and we are not in class together as we are all working from home ... the samples show how different groups have done the activity in different ways... so we can watch the samples given to us and have some ideas on doing it."

(Student 1)

"No, I think it will give me more pressure. Some of the samples were done well, the technical aspects were good and there were similar styles that were used in the production. For me, not providing samples is better because once I see the sample it will make me think I should do like that instead of brainstorming to make my own idea. Sometimes I am afraid that the samples may influence our ideas and the creativity will lose."

(Student 7)

4.4.2 Challenges of the task

To answer Research Question 2, 'What are the challenges faced by the students in completing the Vlog task?', the interview conducted revealed the following issues.

4.4.2.1 Technological skills

All the interviewees agreed that technical and creative skills are crucial for this task because they had to do editing to ensure the video turned out interesting and was able to impress the audience. They believed that, without editing, their video would be simple and boring. They had to use the up-to-date applications and techniques in editing their videos. Thus, some students shared that preparing a Vlog was not that easy because they needed certain technological skills.

The majority of the interviewees concurred that the lecturer did not need to equip them with technical and creative skills as they preferred independent learning and were able to explore those skills on their own when given freedom to choose the software or application that they preferred. Some of them said that tips given were enough for them to explore on their own. A minority of the interviewees, however, responded that the lecturer should have exposed them to technological skills as a preparation for this assignment because those skills were needed in completing the task. Some of the students' views are:

"In my opinion, I don't think my lecturer needs to expose technical skills in her lecture as preparation for this assignment. I think many of us use social media to put up many posts. Many of the users are making videos and there are many different types of software and applications. It is good for us to explore different applications and see which ones are easy to be used in the Vlog activity. We ourselves must learn some technical skills as we can use them in our lessons and work."

(Student 1)

"Yes, some of the students might have zero knowledge about technological skills. There are many things for students to learn, especially when we are not very fluent in the language. We are learning new words and learning to speak properly... and we also have to make sure the Vlog looks good as we are sharing with others when we upload it... some of us are not that good at filming and editing... so it would be good if the lecturer gave more practice in basic technical skills."

(Student 8)

4.4.3 Suggestions for improvements

Many suggestions were given by the students as alternatives to making Vlogs. Some suggested that the speaking presentations should be done online and the camera should be on, so everyone can see the presenter's expressions and gestures. It could also avoid the presenters from reading their scripts. They also suggested a forum or talk show on a specific topic that could be done as a live performance. In addition, there was a suggestion for a storytelling video based on non-fiction books. This was almost similar to another suggestion to broaden the types of genres and formats for the students to choose, such as podcast, news, role-play, and musicals in order to promote creativity among students for this assignment. The different choices were important to students so that they would feel comfortable and creative in completing the assignment. Some participants claimed that Vlog was the best assignment for speaking skills as they felt the current situation of COVID-19 pandemic posed many difficulties to creative ideas, specifically when movement control regulations limited outdoor activities:

"I think you can broaden the types of video that students can choose to do... maybe students can do podcasts, news, role play, musicals, and many more... Some of us have many talents and it can be different when not limited. We can still learn the language when we are having fun doing what we are good at and we can see different ideas coming from the groups... as students get to express their creativity..."

(Student 6)

"Considering the current situation of COVID-19, I think for the speaking activities it is better to be done through live video, or video call, or maybe in the google meet. For me, it is important we pay attention to our language learning... the way we use words, our

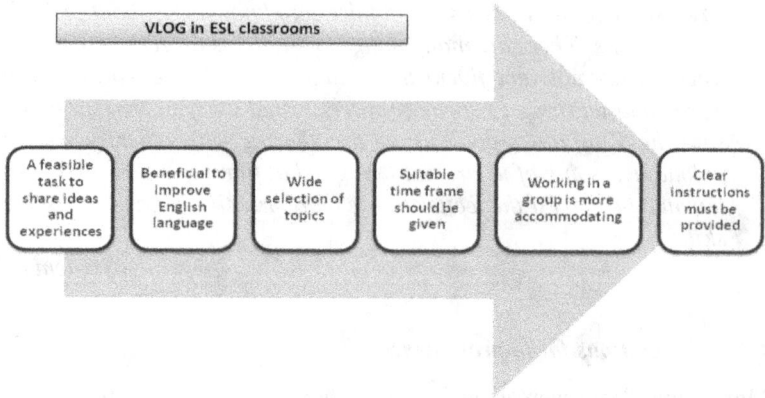

Figure 4.1 Summary of students' experience of using Vlog as a learning tool in ESL classrooms.

> *pronunciation and expressions when we do the speaking. In some of the Vlog activities, we can see that students have spent more time on technical parts… but they are reading from the script… this affects their presentation skills, their expression and gestures because we are paying more attention to recording the video."*
>
> *(Student 7)*

Figure 4.1 summarises the experience of using Vlog among the students in ESL classroom based on the findings in this study.

4.5 Conclusion

Based on the findings, it can be concluded that Vlog could provide positive experience for ESL students in completing a speaking task during times of crises which require online teaching and learning. Vlog was seen as a feasible and interesting way of engaging students with technologies which play important parts in their everyday learning and living. Although both students and their instructors were suddenly pushed to face many uncertainties, the students managed to successfully complete this task and improved their speaking skills. Further, they also gained production skills and learnt about teamwork.

At the end of the task, the students felt positive and productive as they were able to cooperate and make good decisions in topic selection, learning technical skills, peer evaluations on their practices in speaking skills, and interacting with their instructors in a very test-ing time. However, it is asserted here that the instructors must also play their roles in ensuring appropriate time frame is given. Clear and detailed instructions are also helpful to support student learning, and suitable samples are shared with the students to encourage creativity. Continuous communication as witnessed in the weekly feedback sessions between students and instructors in the present study is also an important point.

Despite the constructive feedback received from the students, it was obvious that technological skills were the biggest challenge for them in completing their Vlog. Thus, the instructors need to decide if they would like to expose the students to certain software packages or applications or allow students to explore programs that they feel comfortable using for their projects. At the same time, the instructors must remember that the purpose of this task is to assess their speaking skills, not their technical skills. Apart from that, instructions could also be an issue for some students particularly in terms of the clarity. This was due to the nature of online classes conducted, as some students might be listening to the explanation given by the instructors and some others might be doing something else at home that cannot be observed. Nevertheless, new technologies and disruptive classroom practices are issues that will need serious attention in ESL classrooms in current times.

Post-COVID realities and possibilities

The pandemic has encouraged educators to explore alternative approaches for the teaching and learning process. The significance of the Internet which served as the main bridge to connect educators and learners resulted in post-COVID approaches which can serve in the field of teaching speaking skills. Vlog which is a tool used by students to interact can serve as an alternative approach to boost speaking activities in language learning.

References

Ajoke, A. R. (2017) The Importance of Instructional Materials in Teaching English as A Second Language. *International Journal of Humanities and Social Science Invention.* 6(9), 36–44. Available from: www.ijhssi.org

Alkurtehe, K., Mohan, R. & Krishnasamy, H. (2019) Improve Vocabulary through Watching Videos. *European Academic Research.* 11, 2728–2738.

Anggraeni, A., Rachmijati, C. & Apriliyanti, D. L. (2020) Vlog: A Tool for Students' Speaking Practice Enhancement. *Research and Innovation in Language Learning*. Available from:https://doi.org/10.33603/rill.v3i1.2775.

Codreanu, T. & Combe, C. (2019) Vlogs, Video Publishing, and Informal Language Learning. In *The Handbook of Informal Language Learning*. Available from: https://doi.org/10.1002/9781119472384.ch10.

Eng, L., Saeed, K. & Mohamed Ismail, S. A. M. (2019) Malaysian Speaking Proficiency Assessment Effectiveness for Undergraduates Suffering from Minimal Descriptors. *International Journal of Instruction*. 12, 1059–1076. Available from: https://doi.org/10.29333/iji.2019.12168a

Madzlan, N. A., Seng, G. H. & Kesevan, H. V. (2020) Use of Video Blogs in Alleviating Public speaking Anxiety Among ESL Learners. *Journal of Education and E-Learning Research*. 7(1). Available from: https://doi.org/10.20448/journal.509.2020.71.93.99

Mandasari, B. & Aminatun, D. (2020) Improving Students' Speaking Performance through Vlog. *English Education: Journal of English Teaching and Research*. 5(2), 136–142. Available from: https://doi.org/10.29407/jetar.v5i2.14772

Masofa, I. & Rahmah, N. A. L. (2018) Implementing Vlog for innovation in ELT practices. The 65th TEFLIN International Conference (pp. 172–179).

Maulidah, I. (2018) Vlog: The Mean to Improve Students' Speaking Ability. 145 (Iconelt 2017), 12–15. Available from: https://doi.org/10.2991/iconelt-17.2018.3

Sanford, D. R. (2020) *The Rowman & Littlefield Guide for Peer Tutors*. London, UK: Rowman & Littlefield Publishers.

Syafri, Edi & Endrizal, N. (2020) VLOG: A Tool for Students' Speaking Practise Enhancement. *Journal of Research and Innovation in Language Learning*. 3(1), 23–31.

Tarighat, S. & Khodabakhsh, S. (2016) Mobile-Assisted Language Assessment: Assessing Speaking. *Computers in Human Behavior*. 64, 409–413. Available from: https://doi.org/10.1016/j.chb.2016.07.014

Thulasi Palpanadan, S., Ahmad, I., Eliana Binti Ahmad Zuki, R. & Abdul Samad, N. (2021) Effects of Using Online Approach on Speaking Skills Among Malaysian University Students. *English Literature and Language Review*. 72, 34–38. Available from: https://doi.org/10.32861/ellr.72.34.38

Wulandari, M. (2019) Improving EFL Learners' Speaking Proficiency Through Instagram Vlog. *LLT Journal: A Journal on Language and Language Teaching*. 22(1), 111–125. Available from: doi.org/10.24071/llt.2019.220111

Part B

Corona speak

Issues in language and literacy

5 Foreign language learning at the university

Students' perceptions and emotions

Omar Colombo and Tamara Boscia

5.1. Introduction

The present research was started during the second semester of the academic year 2019/2020 in a Malaysian university and involved students and lecturers of the Bachelors of French and Italian as Foreign Languages (FFL, IFL). The semester was conducted entirely online (April/July), due to the COVID-19 syndrome. For this reason, the researchers of this study, who are also lecturers of French and Italian, find the definition of *Emergency Remote Teaching* (ERT) more appropriate than just distance learning since ERT has its own characteristics, mainly of being temporary by nature and often unplanned, due to circumstances (see Hodges *et al.* 2020). In their research on COVID-19 pandemic and online learning, Olasile and Emrah (2020, p. 2) confirm that "effective online learning is a byproduct of cautious design and planning of instruction with the application of organized models for designing and development of instruction". They agree that the rejection of distance learning as effective online education during the pandemic is due to the lack of cautious design and development process and must be explained within the context of ERT.

To accommodate the requests of ERT, most lecturers of FFL and IFL migrated their courses to the institutional platform *Spectrum*, but frequently used email services or *WhatsApp* to deliver lessons and even tests in case of poor Internet connection. Lecturers remained available during the planned lesson time and throughout the day. Synchronous live-streamed lessons made 25% of the lessons, whereas 75% of the lessons were conducted in asynchronous modality.

By analysing learners' perceptions and emotions of their learning experience during the COVID-19 emergency, this study aimed to examine both distance learning in the academic year 2020/2021 and post-pandemic blended teaching and learning. Studies have recently

DOI: 10.4324/9781003182733-7

been conducted on distance learning during COVID-19 pandemic; however, this study was the first one to explore learners' perceptions and emotions of distance foreign language learning (DFLL) in FFL and IFL, in a Malaysian higher educational environment during this emergency.

Three main research questions (RQ) were employed to guide this study:

RQ1: How did learners perceive the online course? Were they satisfied with the course as a whole?
RQ2: Were learners' emotions mostly positive or negative?
RQ3: Were students' DFLL perceptions and emotions correlated with their individual characteristics?

5.2 Literature review

5.2.1 Studies on students' learning perceptions

Research in the field of adult and university education shows that individual factors and digital learning environment (DLE) can affect student learning quality (Charlier *et al.* 2015), outcomes, DLE perception, and satisfaction. A positive learners' perception of DLE generates a positive learning attitude (self-efficacy) and a positive perception of learning (task value: see below) and outcomes (Charlier *et al.* 2015).

According to Lee Watson and Kim (2016, p. 274), learning attitude "consists of three components – affective, cognitive and behavioural – which are closely aligned with [one] another and create a stable perception of a given object or concept". For instance, *task value* (TV) is "the learners' perceptions of the interest, usefulness, importance, and cost of a task, as a factor to predict the learners' decision to further follow the task or not" (Ghasemi and Dowlatabadi 2018, p. 665). TV "is connected to closer or more remote aims, beyond one's immediate pleasure" (Cocoradă and Maican 2021, p. 4). Furthermore, TV is a learning attitude that influences the students' outcomes, learning strategies, and motivation: "when the required skills are higher than the students' skills and students perceive the task as useful, they feel fear or anxiety" (Cocoradă and Maican 2021, p. 3). As for the students' perception of TV, the instructors' behaviours may influence FL learning, given that "the more negative the students' perception [of the teacher's role] is, the more anxious the students will be" (Cocoradă and Maican 2021, p. 4).

More precisely, the interactionist theory of *Transactional Distance* (TD) analyses collaborative interactions in a specific learning context, between students on one hand, and peers, teachers, teaching/learning design, and content on the other hand. A study conducted by Kara (2020) on Turkish learners' perception and satisfaction of an English DFLL context states that students' satisfaction with the DFLL was linearly correlated with the attitudes towards interpersonal interaction. Satisfaction was higher when the instructor had a positive attitude towards interaction, and lower when there was a lack of teachers' encouragement of peer interaction. Similarly, Li and Xu (2019) and Dewaele and MacIntyre (2019) yielded that the higher the positive emotional atmosphere created by the instructors (like a friendly environment), the higher the FL enjoyment. Furthermore, Dewaele *et al.* (2019) clarify that teachers play a more significant role in the student enjoyment than students' peer relationships.

5.2.2 Studies on students' learning emotions

As we have seen, (D)FLL context can affect both learners' positive and negative emotions. In turn, pleasant and unpleasant emotions may influence the students' foreign language (FL) experience (Dewaele *et al.* 2017) and outcomes. The most studied emotion in FLL is anxiety, commonly described as the negative emotional reaction aroused when learning or using an FL. Anxiety is detrimental to the learning process (Boudreau *et al.* 2018), it is correlated with cognitive disruptions and associated with self-focused thinking (Norton and Abbott 2016), feelings of tension, apprehension, nervousness, and worry (Leigh 2015). Conversely, positive emotions are considered beneficial to learning (Boudreau *et al.* 2018). FLL enjoyment may even serve a protective function against negative emotions, like language anxiety, when it cannot be avoided (Dewaele *et al.* 2019, MacIntyre 2017). However, in their study of FLL enjoyment and anxiety of 1746 multilingual students around the world, Dewaele and MacIntyre (2014) showed that the two dependent variables were negatively correlated, but that they shared less than 13% of their variance. They were not the two ends of the same emotional continuum, but two distinct feelings with specific dynamics, the trend of which could occasionally converge or diverge.

5.2.3 Studies on students' learning perceptions and emotions during COVID-19 pandemic

Among recent studies that focused on students' perceptions and emotions of online learning in higher education during COVID-19 pandemic, Rohman *et al.* (2020) showed that even if distance learning is usually one of the encouraging substitutes of class-based courses, students yielded a negative perception of their distance learning experience (Rohman *et al.* 2020), which could also lead to psychological distress (Bao and Hasan 2020).

A study conducted by Cocoradă and Maican in 2021 shares the same focus as this study, since it aimed to observe 207 Romanian learners' behaviour, perceptions, and emotions during the COVID-19 pandemic in a DFLL context. With regard to learners' perceptions, Cocoradă and Maican (2021) showed that the lowest (Likert scale) scores of the perceived TV concerned the individualized teacher feedback, since the teacher's feedback was generally delayed in DLE compared to class-based environment. Cocoradă and Maican (2021) reckoned that their study findings "are consistent with other [pre-pandemic] studies which reveal that mixed feelings in L2 communication are detected in relation to specific events. The pandemic is a traumatic event and online learning is a complex process, in which the chances to succeed or fail are present, but uncertain" (Cocoradă and Maican 2021, p. 15). More precisely, in their study, learners' DFLL enjoyment and anxiety feelings were directly associated, negatively correlated but dynamically coexistent, and enjoyment held a protective role against stressors (anxiety). The authors stated that despite their general enjoyment of DFLL during the pandemic, students preferred blended learning to full online courses. Indeed, students were troubled by poor Internet connection problems, overload of assignments and tasks, lack of interaction with teachers and peers, and concern about FL progression.

5.2.4 Studies on impact of students' characteristics on students' perceptions and emotions

Finally, as for the correlation between student's individual characteristics, perceptions, satisfaction, and emotions, Altugan (2015) stated that the student cultural profile (ethnic, social, linguistic, and economic variables) is linked with (D)FLL: e.g. cultural features could discourage learners' identification with the target FL and culture and, hence, decrease FLL motivation. Dewaele and MacIntyre (2014) showed that the higher the number of languages known, the mastery of the target FL and the educational level, the higher the enjoyment, and the lower the anxiety. With regard to the positive role played by the learners' educational profile, Kara (2020) stated that the perception of TV and the instructional TD was affected by the students' previous technological knowledge. Furthermore, Cocoradă and Maican (2021) showed that anxiety was more common in learners with higher perceived TV and with lower previous online environment knowledge. Cocoradă and Maican (2021) showed also that learners' gender, study program, and achievement level did not affect learners' perceptions and emotions of DFLL during the COVID-19 pandemic. This last result seems in contradiction with other recent studies: for instance, Qiu *et al.* (2020) state that Chinese females reported higher distress than males in DFLL during the same pandemic.

5.3 Method

5.3.1 Data collection

Data was collected using two surveys, one on perceptions and one on positive and negative emotions experienced during the DFLL by 78 students of French and Italian courses who voluntarily chose to participate in the survey. The online questionnaires were designed with *Google Forms*. Over the last week of the DFLL (June 2020), IFL and FFL learners received a link to the surveys via *WhatsApp*. Learners' assessment was based on a five-point Likert scale from 1 (*strongly disagree*) to 5 (*strongly agree*). By filling out the questionnaire anonymously, respondents granted permission to analyse data for the purpose of the research. Given the small sample size of this study case, its findings cannot be generalized.

5.3.2 Perception survey

The final version of the DFLL perception survey (20 items) was an adaptation of the one proposed by Young and Norgard (2006). Five items were grouped in each of the four categories: learner preference regarding the course structure/design (category 1), course TD (online learner/learner and learner/teacher interactions; category 2), course TV (content and assessment; category 3), learner preference regarding online versus traditional face-to face courses, autonomy and satisfaction with their DFLL experience (category 4).

5.3.3 Emotion survey

The survey on emotions (34 items) was based on the questionnaire proposed by Dewaele and MacIntyre (2014), whose study focus was similar to that of this research. The *Distance language Learning Positive Emotions* (DLPE) category was composed of four subcategories and 21 statements: feelings of self-confidence (subcategory 1, 6 items), feeling of enjoyment (subcategory 2, 4 items), motivational feelings in following DFLL (subcategory 3, 3 items), and appreciation of the interpersonal collaboration (subcategory 4, 8 items). As for the *Distance language Learning Negative Emotions* (DLNE), the three subcategories consisted of 13 statements: anxiety feelings related to the student performance during the DFLL (subgroup 5, 6 statements) lack of self-confidence (subgroup 6, 5 statements), and frustration at having technological and Internet accessibility problems (subcategory 7, 2 statements).

5.3.4 Instrument and procedure

For this database analysis, a few statistical tests were performed using SPSS together with a descriptive statistical analysis of the learners' scores, means (M) and standard deviation (SD). Each test had a minimum level of significance of $p = 0.05$ (two-tailed). The dependent variables (DVs) were correlated with six individual factors (independent variables, IVs) grouped in three categories: sociocultural (ethnicity; gender), linguistic competence (mastery of the target FL; number of languages known, NLK; MUET, *Malaysian University Entrance Test*, English as a FL certificate results), and educational (previous or no previous distance learning experience). Researchers performed One-Way ANOVA tests, Paired Sample *t* test (for descriptive statistics in analysing the mean and SD variances), and linear correlation tests (Pearson, *r*; Eta Squared coefficient test, eta^2) between DVs and IVs, as well as between and within the DVs. Finally, two learner dichotomous nominal variables, gender and previous/no previous distance learning experience, were correlated with the DV by an Independent *t* (*t value*) test.

5.3.5 Availability of data and materials

The datasets generated and/or analysed during the current study are not publicly available due to individual privacy reasons. Nevertheless, the original surveys are available from the corresponding author upon request.

5.4 Findings and discussion

5.4.1 Participants' background

The 78 learners that completed the DFLL surveys were enrolled in the bachelor of FFL (50%, N = 39) and IFL (50%, N = 39). With regard to the educational profile, most students had no previous experience with distance learning (70.5%, N = 55). As for the respondents' sociocultural information, students were mostly females (87.2%, N = 68), and belonged to the Malay ethnical-cultural group (62.8%, N = 49). As for the learners' linguistic background, learners were multilingual (native and foreign languages): they spoke more than two languages, the majority were quadrilingual or pentalingual (55.1% in total, N = 43). Since the learners were enrolled in the first or the second year (74.4%, N = 58), 82.1% of them rated their mastery of FFL or IFL as low intermediate (level A2) or intermediate (B1). Lastly, most of the students (87.2%, N = 68) obtained band 3 or 4 in the MUET certificate. See Table 5.1 for the respondents' sociocultural and linguistic background details.

5.4.2 Overall findings of learners' DFLL perceptions

This section looks at the learner perceptions of the DFLL course during COVID-19 (RQ1).

Table 5.2 shows similar moderate means of the four categories, with an overall mean of 3.59. Results also yield a similar Likert distribution (SD). Learners were appreciative of the DFLL course structure (category 1) as well as the interpersonal relationships during online learning (TD, category 2), while expressing a lower level of satisfaction for the DFLL course as a whole (category 4). A series of Paired sample *t* tests confirmed the general lower value given to distance learning satisfaction at the end of the course: the most important mean-variance was between satisfaction and, on the other hand, structure/design,

Table 5.1 Student participants from distance learning of French and Italian as foreign languages (FFL/IFL) (N = 78)

Ethnic groups	Languages known	Mastery of FFL/IFL	MUET
Malay: 62.8%	Three languages: 23%	Beginner: 15.4%	Band 2: 1.3%
Chinese: 21.8%	Four languages: 25.6%	Low-intermediate: 44.9%	Band 3: 35.9%
Kadazandusun: 5.1%	Five languages: 29.5%	Intermediate: 37.2%	Band 4: 51.3%
Indian: 5.1%	Six languages: 15.5%	Upper-intermediate: 2.5%	Band 5: 11.5%
Other[a]: 5.2%	Seven/eight languages: 6.4%	Advanced: 0%	Band 6: 0%

[a] Other: Bisaya, Bruneian, Dusun, and Sungai.

Table 5.2 Statistics of students' perceptions on distance foreign
language learning (DFLL)

Category (N = 78)		M	DM[a]	SD	DSD[b]
1) Online course structure/design		3.74	0.39	0.55	1.14
2) Online course TD[c]		3.70		0.63	
3) Online course TV[d]		3.56		0.65	
4) Satisfaction		3.35		0.43	
Paired sample *t* test (df = 77)				t	p
Satisfaction	Online course structure/design			−5.45	0.00
(DFLL[e] course as a	Online course TD[c]			−5.27	
whole)	Online course TV[d]			−3.06	
Paired – Correlation Pearson test				r	p
Online course TD[c]	Online course TV[d]			0.48	0.00
(interpersonal	Online course structure/design			0.42	
interactions)	Satisfaction			0.35	
Online course TV[d]	Satisfaction			0.35	

[a] Difference mean.
[b] Difference SD.
[c] Transactional distance.
[d] Task value.
[e] Distance foreign language learning.

TD, and TV. Moreover, the relevance of TD was corroborated by a
Pearson correlation test that linked the TD linearly with the three
other sections: the higher the value given to interpersonal relationships, the higher the appreciation of TV, course structure/design, and
final DFLL satisfaction. In addition, the higher the TV, the higher the
course satisfaction.

In response to RQ1, it may be concluded that despite a general lower
appreciation of the DFLL course, in line with the findings of Rohman
et al. (2020), the learners with the highest level of satisfaction perceived
the DFLL classes as interesting and useful (TV) and, as in the findings
of Kara (2020), highly valued interpersonal collaboration (TD).

5.4.3 Overall findings of learners' DFLL emotions

5.4.3.1 Overall findings between learners' DLPE and DLNE

With regards to learners' emotions (RQ2), a general overview of
the data (see Table 5.3) showed many similarities between learners'
DLPE and DLNE categories as a whole. The distribution of the Likert
scores between learners' positive and negative emotions was similar.
Nevertheless, a Pearson correlation test yielded a moderate negative

Table 5.3 Statistics of students' distance learning positive and negative emotions (DLPE/DLNE)

Category	Overall findings (N = 78)				Paired sample t test (df = 77)		Pearson correlation	
	M^a	SD	DM^a	DSD^b	t	p	r	p
DLPE	3.65	0.58	−0.03	1.00	−0.28	0.78	−0.26	0.02
DLNE	3.68	0.63						

[a] Difference mean.
[b] Difference SD.

correlation between the two opposite feelings: the higher the learner's scores on DLPE, the lower the scores on DLNE, and vice versa.

Indeed, Table 5.4 states that in terms of the major mean differences between the opposite learners' DLPE/DLNE subgroups, Paired sample *t* tests showed that despite a high motivation for DFLL course as a whole, learners felt less enjoyment and negative emotions of frustration (due to poor Internet connection) and anxiety (as regards the student's FL performance). More details within learners' DLPE and DLNE categories will be presented in the next section. Furthermore, correlation tests also confirmed inverse linear intergroup correlations: learners that enjoyed the DFLL felt a lower level of anxiety

Table 5.4 Overall statistics of students' positive and negative emotions on DFLL

Paired	Overall findings (N = 78)				Paired sample t test (df = 77)		Pearson correlation	
	M^a	SD	DM^a	DSD^b	t	p	r	p
Motivation	4.02	0.63	0.63	1.05	4.57	0.00	−0.27	0.01
Lack of SC[c]	3.39	0.84						
Enjoyment	3.21	0.87	−0.80	1.24	−5.01		−0.31	0.00
Frustration	4.01	0.89						
Enjoyment	3.21	0.87	−0.60	1.17	−4.16		−0.23	0.01
Anxiety	3.81	0.78						
Interpers. Coll.[d]	3.79	0.64	0.40	1.06	2.89		−0.25	0.01
Lack of SC[c]	3.39	0.84						

[a] Difference mean.
[b] Difference SD.
[c] Lack of self-confidence.
[d] Interpersonal collaboration.

and frustration. Similarly, the higher the lack of self-confidence, the lower the learner motivation for DFLL and satisfaction with their interpersonal collaboration.

In response to RQ2, the general emotional variance in terms of learners' DLPE and DLNE assessment was not statistically significant (see DLPE and DLNE final means and SDs), even though each learner experienced mainly positive or mainly negative emotions, which, in line with previous studies (Cocoradă and Maican 2021, Dewaele and MacIntyre 2014), appeared to be in an inverse linear correlation with each other.

5.4.3.2 Overall findings within learners' DLPE and DLNE

The purpose of this section is to observe the emotional variance among learners' DLPE and DLNE subgroups (RQ2).

Findings within DLPE (see Table 5.5): The overall means of the four DLPE subgroups were high, i.e. with a moderate difference mean and a small dispersion (SD). The most positive emotions involved learners' motivation to attend the DFLL classes, while general enjoyment was lower.

In contrast to the findings of Cocoradă and Maican (2021), it may be concluded that students' DLPE were supported primarily by the motivation to learn the target FL rather than by their general DFLL course enjoyment. Finally, Pearson tests showed a higher linear positive association between the four positive feelings: self-confidence, enjoyment, motivation, and appreciation of interpersonal collaboration tended to increase homogeneously (r value between 0.46 and 0.73, $p < 0.05$).

Table 5.5 Statistics of students' positive emotions on DFLL

Category ($N = 78$)	M	DM^a	SD	DSD^b
1) Motivation	4.02	0.81	0.63	1.38
2) Interpersonal collaboration	3.79		0.64	
3) Self-confidence	3.39		0.84	
4) Enjoyment	3.21		0.87	
Paired sample *t* test (df = 77)		DM^a	**t**	**p**
Motivation Enjoyment		0.80	10.14	0.00

[a] Difference mean.
[b] Difference SD.

Table 5.6 Statistics of students' negative emotions on DFLL

Category (N = 78)	M	DM[a]	SD	DSD[b]
1) Frustration	4.01	0.62	0.89	1.45
2) Anxiety	3.81		0.78	
3) Lack of self-confidence	3.39		0.84	
Paired sample *t* test (df = 77)		**DM**[a]	**t**	**p**
Frustration　　Lack of self-confidence		0.62	5.18	0.00

[a] Difference mean.
[b] Difference SD.

Findings within DLNE (see Table 5.6): Similar to the DLPE subgroups statistical trend, the overall means were high, with a moderate difference mean and a general small dispersion. Stronger negative emotions engaged the feelings of frustration due to poor Internet connection and computer disruption, while the general lack of self-confidence as regards personal performance in FL target skills held a lower value.

In line with recent studies on learners' emotions during DFLL courses in COVID-19 times, these findings show that the learners' main concerns were related to the potential unforeseen risk of poor Internet connection and disruption of technological tools, which could affect learning activities. Analogously to the learners' DLPE subgroups, Person tests showed a higher linear positive correlation among students' DLNE subcategories, i.e. anxiety, lack of self-confidence, and frustration (r value between 0.27 and 0.65, $p < 0.05$).

5.4.4 *Effects of learners' characteristics on learners' perceptions, satisfaction, and emotions*

The next stage of this study was to understand whether the individual variables had any effects on learners' perceptions, satisfactions, and emotions (response to RQ3). Three out of six IVs did not yield any influence: learners' gender, MUET certificate result, and perceived FFL/IFL mastery.

Tests showed some significant variance regarding students' language background and only for the learners' online TD perception. Indeed, appreciation for interpersonal collaboration increased by increasing the NLK, which is particularly evident between trilingual on one hand and quadrilingual and pentalingual students on the other hand, that is to say, for most of the learners (61 out of 78 learners, 78% in total; see Table 5.7).

Table 5.7 Correlations between FFL/IFL distance learners' factors and perceptions (N = 78)

Variables		One-way ANOVA				Correlation
IV	DV	df	F	p	η_p^2	eta^2
NLK	Online course TD	5, 72	3.01	0.02	0.17	0.52
Most relevant overall group findings				N	M	SD
Number Languages Known/Online course TD						
Trilingual				18	3.30	0.65
Quadrilingual				20	3.84	0.52
Pentalingual				23	3.80	0.72

η_p^2: Partial Eta Squared test.
eta^2: Eta Squared coefficient test.

As regards to learners' DLPE during the DFLL, Table 5.8 shows that the educational background influenced both enjoyment and self-confidence feelings: students with no previous experience of online courses got more enjoyment and were more self-confident.

Concerning students' DLNE, a One-Way ANOVA test shows that sociocultural belonging impacted learners' lack of self-confidence of their skills in the target FL (see Table 5.9). Precisely, Tukey and Dunnett post hoc tests showed that Chinese students felt less confident than Malay learners.

Table 5.8 Correlations between learners' factors and DLPE subcategories (Independent sample test; df = 76)

Variables		Overall findings (N = 78)			Independent sample test (df = 76)	
IV	DV	N	M	SD	t	p
POE[a]	Enjoyment	23	2.93	0.78	−1.86	0.05
WPOE[b]		55	3.33	0.89		
POE[a]	Self-confidence	23	3.37	0.65	−2.26	0.03
WPOE[b]		55	3.69	0.54		

[a] (With) Previous online experience.
[b] Without Previous online experience.

Table 5.9 Correlations between FFL/IFL distance learners' factors and DLNE subcategories (N = 78)

Variables			One-way ANOVA			Correlation
IV	DV	df	F	p	η_p^2	eta²
Ethnicity	Lack of SC	4, 73	2.30	0.05	0.11	0.33
Most relevant overall group findings				**N**	**M**	**SD**
Ethnicity/lack of self-confidence						
Malay				49	3.23	0.77
Chinese				17	3.92	0.83

η_p^2: Partial Eta Squared test.
eta²: Eta Squared coefficient test.
Lack of SC: Lack of self-confidence.

5.5 Discussion

5.5.1 *Impact of ERT on learners' psychological status: frustration, motivation, satisfaction*

The results of the two surveys show clear contradictory aspects: ERT held a negative impact on learners' psychological and emotional status, with a clear feeling of frustration caused by Internet connection and computer disruption, but it did not affect learners' FLL motivation, which stayed high notwithstanding the forced circumstances. Furthermore, learners showed satisfaction with the course structure/design, even though ERT left lecturers with very little time to design their course.

5.5.2 *Relationship between DLPE and DLNE*

The high level of satisfaction attributed to online interpersonal communication with fellow students and lecturers (TD) can explain why there is a balance between positive and negative emotions: on one hand, frustration and stress might have generated a feeling of lack of self-confidence and general disappointment with the course as a whole; on the other hand, positive feelings are the result of the positive perception of relationships, course design, and TV. The study shows a strong relationship between learners' positive and negative emotions that do not exclude each other and highlights that the two DVs are negatively correlated, as stated by Dewaele and MacIntyre (2014) and Cocoradă and Maican (2021). Additionally, the present research confirms the findings of recent educational studies (Dewaele and MacIntyre 2019, Dewaele *et al.* 2019, Kara 2020, Li and Xu 2019) on the linear correlation between students' satisfaction and interpersonal interaction attitudes: learners' satisfaction of the DFLL as a whole was higher when learners were satisfied with (online) interpersonal interactions.

5.5.3 Impact of learners' characteristics

Learners' characteristics did not play a major role in perceptions and emotions, unlike some study findings mentioned in the theoretical framework of reference for this study. Indeed, Dewaele and MacIntyre (2014) context study was based on a blended learning environment, not an ERT context, which is a major difference. As for this research, regarding linguistic competence, NLK positively affected the appreciation of interpersonal collaboration. Furthermore, the analysis of sociocultural belonging variables disclosed that Chinese students felt less confident than Malay learners. This result is surprising since Chinese students are the ones who know the most languages. Finally, based on the present findings, enjoyment and self-confidence were higher when students had no previous experience of distance learning. This last result appears to contradict other studies, which indicated that previous experience of distance learning had a positive influence on the perception of TV and TD (study of Kara, 2020), but it could indicate that students with previous distance learning knowledge were able to compare that experience with the new ERT, which was not chosen but imposed upon them and was often linked to network issues or the lack of appropriate technology.

5.6 Conclusion

Right now (academic year 2020/2021), universities in Malaysia and in many parts of the world are still conducting their courses online. Despite the many problems related to ERT which are yet to be solved, e.g. human intrusion (like crowded houses, family responsibilities – Olasile and Emrah 2020), poor Internet and outdated technological devices, we can assume that both students and lecturers have increased their self-confidence in learning and teaching. Following the results of this study, which highlighted the importance of interpersonal interaction in the e-learning environment, the lecturers have improved DFLL by increasing the number of synchronous online face-to face lessons. As stated by Blum (2020), videoconferencing resembles real life, making it possible to hear voices and exchange information and views.

Taking this into consideration, in future blended learning, attention must be placed on the constant monitoring of the task assigned to offer students continuous constructive feedback, also when working with asynchronous video-based flipped learning. Course design has been improved by designing more collaborative and interactive tasks and equipping students with the tools to help them become more independent learners. Videoconferencing, break-out rooms, and chats have proved to be effective in fostering peer communication and interaction. Even in future blended learning environments, interaction must be the keyword when designing materials and tasks. This will work in the direction of lowering the feeling of anxiety some learners experience when engaging in FL learning. In order to decrease the students' feeling of frustration due to network problems, the lecturers have set more flexible deadlines, and this should also be done in a blended environment. Since students' FLL motivation remained high throughout the ERT, the lecturers have continued to enhance it by maintaining a friendly and supportive environment, by designing achievable tasks and, as said above, by extending deadlines. In a post-COVID environment, blended learning can support student motivation by offering an efficient online space for further learning.

Research is needed to analyse students' feelings and perceptions after one year of ERT and lecturers' perceptions and feelings throughout the whole period of ERT and after one year. The results of these new studies will eventually significantly improve blended learning in a post COVID-19 learning and teaching environment.

Post-COVID realities and possibilities

Hybrid learning will probably become the norm in higher education institutions in the post COVID-19 era. The valuable first-hand experience universities have acquired during ERT could guide and inform this transition. A student-centred learning approach should be adopted in both online and face-to face settings. This would enhance the learning process and place interaction at its core, so that the student's perceptions and emotions related to learning will not hamper but foster effective learning and personal growth.

List of abbreviations

(D)FLL	(Distance) foreign language learning.
DLE	Digital learning environment.
DLNE	Distance language learning negative emotions.
DLPE	Distance language learning positive emotions.
DV(s)	Dependent variable(s).
ERT	Emergency remote teaching.
FFL	French as a foreign language.
FL	Foreign language.
IFL	Italian as a foreign language.
IV(s)	Independent variable(s).
M	Mean(s).
MUET	Malaysian University Entrance Test.
NLK	Number of languages known.
RQ	Research question(s).
SD	Standard deviation.
TD	Transactional distance.
TV	Task value.

References

Altugan, A., 2015. The relationship between cultural identity and learning. *Procedia-Social and Behavioral Sciences*, 186, 1159–1162. DOI: 10.1016/j. sbspro.2015.04.161.

Bao, Y. and Hasan, N., 2020. Impact of "e-Learning crack-up" perception on psychological distress among college students during COVID-19 pandemic: A mediating role of "fear of academic year loss". *Children and Youth Services Review*, 118, 105355. DOI: https://doi.org/10.1016/j.childyouth.2020.105355.

Blum, S.D., 2020. Why we're exhausted by Zoom. Inside Higher Ed. [online]. Available from: https://www.insidehighered.com/advice/2020/04/22/professor-explores-why-zoom-classes-deplete-her-energy-opinion [Accessed 10 April 2021].

Boudreau, C., Dewaele, J.M., and MacIntyre, P.D., 2018. Enjoyment and anxiety in second language communication: An idiodynamic approach. *Studies in Second Language Learning and Teaching*, 8 (1), 149–170. DOI: 10.14746/ssllt.2018.8.1.7.

Charlier, B., Cosnefroy, L., Jézégou, A., and Lameul, G., 2015. Understanding Quality of Learning in Digital Learning Environments: State of the Art and Research Needed. In: A. Curaj, L. Matei, R. Pricopie, J. Salmi, and P. Scott, eds. *The European Higher Education Area*. Cham: Springer, 381–398. DOI: 10.1007/978-3-319-20877-0_25.

Cocoradă, E. and Maican, M.A., 2021. Online foreign language learning in higher education and its correlates during the COVID-19 pandemic. *Sustainability*, 13(781), 1–21. DOI: 10.3390/su13020781.

Dewaele, J.M. and MacIntyre, D.P., 2014. The two faces of Janus? Anxiety and enjoyment in the foreign language classroom. *Studies in Second Language Learning and Teaching, 4/2, Special issue: Positive Psychology*, 4(2), 237–274. DOI: 10.14746/ssllt.2014.4.2.5.

Dewaele, J.M. and MacIntyre, D.P., 2019. The predictive power of multicultural personality traits, learner and teacher variables on foreign language enjoyment and anxiety. In: S. Masatoshi and L. Shawn, eds. *Evidence-Based Second Language Pedagogy*. Abington: Routledge, 263–286. DOI: 10.4324/9781351190558.

Dewaele, J.M., Witney, J., Saito, K., and Dewaele, L., 2017. Foreign language enjoyment and anxiety: The effect of teacher and learner variables. *Language Teaching Research*, 22, 676–697. DOI: 10.1177/1362168817692161.

Dewaele, J.M., Chen, X., Padilla, A.M., and Lake, J., 2019. The flowering of positive psychology in foreign language teaching and acquisition research. *Frontiers in Psychology*, 10, 2128. [online]. Available from: https://www.frontiersin.org/articles/10.3389/fpsyg.2019.02128/full [Accessed 15 April 2021].

Ghasemi, A.A. and Dowlatabadi, H.R., 2018. Investigating the role of task value, surface/deep learning strategies, and higher order thinking in predicting self-regulation and language achievement. *The Journal of Asia TEFL*, 15(3), 664–681. DOI: 10.18823/asiatefl.2018.15.3.7.664.

Hodges, C., Moore, S., Lockee, B., Trust, T., and Bond, A., 2020. The difference between emergency remote teaching and online learning. Educause Review [online]. Available from: https://er.educause.edu/articles/2020/3/the-difference-between-emergency-remote-teaching-and-online-learning [Accessed 8 January 2021].

Kara, M., 2020. Transactional distance and learner outcomes in an online EFL context. *Open Learning: The Journal of Open, Distance and e-Learning*, 36(1), 45–60. DOI: 10.1080/02680513.2020.1717454.

Lee Watson, S., and Kim, W., 2016. Enrolment purposes, instructional activities, and perceptions of attitudinal learning in a human trafficking MOOC. *Open Learning: The Journal of Open, Distance and e-Learning*, 31(3), 273–287. DOI: 10.1080/02680513.2016.1230845.

Leigh, H., 2015. Anxiety and Anxiety Disorders. In: H. Leigh and J. Streltzer, eds. *Handbook of Consultation-Liaison Psychiatry*, 2nd ed. New York: Springer Science + Business Media, 213–224. DOI: 10.1007/978-3-319-11005-9.

Li, C. and Xu, J., 2019. Trait emotional intelligence and classroom emotions: A positive psychology investigation and intervention among Chinese EFL learners. *Frontiers in Psychology*, 10, 2453. [Online]. Available from: https://www.frontiersin.org/articles/10.3389/fpsyg.2019.02453/full [Accessed 12 April 2021].

MacIntyre, P.D., 2017. An Overview of Language Anxiety Research and Trends in its Development. In: C. Gkonou, L. Daubney, and J.M. Dewaele, eds. *New Insights into Language Anxiety: Theory, Research and Educational Implications*. Bristol: Multilingual Matters, 11–30. DOI: 10.21832/9781783097722-003.

Norton, A.R. and Abbott, M.J., 2016. Self-focused cognition in social anxiety: A review of the theoretical and empirical literature. *Behaviour Change*, 33 (1), 44–64. DOI: 10.1017/bec.2016.2.

Olasile, B.A. and Emrah, S., 2020. Covid-19 pandemic and online learning: the challenges and opportunities, Interactive Learning Environments. *Interactive Learning Environments*, 1–13. DOI: 10.1080/10494820.2020.1813180.

Qiu, J., Shen, B., Zhao, M., Wang, Z., Xie, B., and Xu, Y., 2020. A nationwide survey of psychological distress among Chinese people in the COVID-19 epidemic: Implications and policy recommendations. *General Psychiatry*, 33 (2), e100213. [online]. Available from: https://gpsych.bmj.com/content/33/2/e100213 [Accessed 13 April 2021].

Rohman, M., Marji, D.A.S., Sugandi, R.M., and Nurhadi, D., 2020. Online learning in higher education during covid-19 pandemic: Students' perceptions. *Journal of Talent Development and Excellence*, 12 (2s), 3644–3651.

Young, A. and Norgard, C., 2006. Assessing the quality of online courses from the students' perspective. *The Internet and Higher Education*, 9, 107–115. DOI: 10.1016/j.iheduc.2006.03.001.

6 A morphological analysis of COVID-19 novel words used in Malaysia

Komalata Manokaran, Shyi Nian Ong, and Rodney C. Jubilado

6.1 Introduction

6.1.1 Background of the study

The COVID-19 crisis has made 2020 an unprecedented year of large-scale learning in the world. In January 2020, when the novel coronavirus outbreak in Wuhan, China, made international headlines, the disease it caused had not even been discovered, and shortly after that, COVID-19 became a global pandemic. The name of the disease did not even exist before February 2020. The name of the coronavirus disease entered the vocabulary of the vast majority of the world's 8 billion people. COVID-19 has likely entered the vocabulary project of the largest number of language databases in the shortest time. However, understanding the names of new diseases constitutes only a small part of the mass communication related to the pandemic. Almost everyone in the world must learn public health concepts, such as *social distancing, lockdown,* or *flattening the curve* to avoid infection. Almost everyone must understand the details of containment measures such as lockdowns, contact tracing, or mask-wearing in their jurisdiction. Everyone has been in contact and has to form views on the often highly divided public debates that weigh the relationship between health and economy, link the virus to specific social groups, or politicise the disease (Piller et al., 2020).

COVID-19 has been declared a pandemic by the World Health Organisation (WHO) as it continues to spread globally. As more countries roll out measures to contain the spread, media coin novel words together with the new disease. Some of the words and ideas associated with the crisis are novel since the COVID-19 calamity has advanced quickly. These words are very new, and others have reviewed definitions; some words are newly conspicuous in the language. The new words are required to increase our vocabulary and meet the pressing

DOI: 10.4324/9781003182733-8

demands of communicating the thought processes related to the pandemic. Word-formations such as acronym, blending, clipping, coining, and compounding are used to acquire novel words.

The morphological aspect of linguistics, namely the process of word formation, can be considered as a new language and use new words (Luthfiyati et al., 2017). Many morphological processes are involved in the formation of novel words during the COVID-19 outbreak in the media. Novel words are coined to provide names for things, processes, situations, and ideologies. Novel words are spreading swiftly among speakers and English users globally due to globalisation and the advances in journalism and the media. It is necessary to classify and acknowledge some of these terms academically by not overlooking the importance of their contribution to the continual process of word-formation in the English and Malay language within the Malaysian context. Malaysian also coined several novel words in conjunction with the pandemic, such as *movement control order (MCO)* instead of lockdown.

6.1.2 Problem statement

The term *social isolation* existed long before the COVID-19 pandemic but became more common in 2020. Both *self-isolate* and *self-isolation* have received new references to illustrate their current usage. The meaning of some terms has changed. Initially, it meant hiding or taking refuge in places where they sought safety during regional events such as tornadoes or *active shooting attacks.* It also pointed to separate from society and its daily activities. It is now used to refer to long periods of social isolation. Correspondingly, *elbow bumps* have evolved from gestures like high-five (recorded in 1981) and evolved into their current form: a safe way to greet others. There are also some regional differences in the COVID-19 language. *Self-isolation* has always been the preferred term in British English, while *self-quarantine* is more commonly used in the United States through its Centre for Disease Control and Prevention. "Rona" is a new term of Coronavirus used in the United States and Australia. Still, many people in Malaysia wonder about the meaning of the coinage during the pandemic.

COVID-19 injects a virus into our living environment and a variant of the language used every day in Malaysia. Before the pandemic, it was rare or not even never – for the media, writing, or conversation to highlight terms related to the pandemic (Harian, 2021). According to Asif et al. (2020), throughout the history of epidemics and pandemics, the coinage of new words has played a significant role. The condition of the coronavirus outbreak is moving fast globally. Broadcast and information about the disease can be distressing due to the confusing new terms used about the outbreak. For example, the Prime Minister of Malaysia addressed the term MCO for the first time during the current pandemic on 25th March 2020 via television broadcast. Understanding the words is essential to help people stay informed and safe; hence, this study will also define and explain the terms associated with the outbreak. Furthermore, the creation of novel words has attracted the attention of linguists to identify the morphological process of those words (e.g. Asif et al., 2020; Akut, 2020).

The world discusses the novel coronavirus outbreak and its devastating impact on countries worldwide. People encounter many medical terms, words, and phrases related to COVID-19 almost every day. Human language is considered the entity of creativity that supports the survival and further development of languages. The fact is that dictionaries in all languages are developing day by day. There are many morphological processes of new words, such as word-formation, as seen in COVID-19, which emerged globally during the outbreak. Coinage of new words is one of the morphological processes used to describe or name a new event, referent, or phenomenon. This study aims to classify the types of morphological processes and to identify the meanings of novel words during the outbreak.

6.1.3 Research objectives

This research has the following objectives:

1 To classify types of morphological processes used in the formation of novel words.
2 To identify the meaning of the novel words.

6.1.4 Research questions

This research aims to answer the following questions:

1 What types of morphological processes are used in the formation of novel words?
2 What is the meaning of the novel words coined during the outbreak?

6.1.5 Significance of the study

This study contributes to the field of morphology in two ways. It will identify and classify word-formation processes and find the meaning of the novel words used during the COVID-19 outbreak. Then, the scholar, society, and readers can use this study to broaden their knowledge of the novel words used during the outbreak and understand their meanings to help the public stay educated and safe.

6.1.6 Limitations of the study

This study focuses on novel words used during the outbreak. Thus, only types and linguistic features will be analysed. Furthermore, only words related to the outbreak are given full attention to the study. The sample size is small because the data collection process has only taken words mainly from *The Star* newspaper (December 2019 to October 2020). Many words were coined during the outbreak globally. However, the vocabulary that was fondly used in Malaysia was analysed in this study. Therefore, the generalisation of the samples is studied prudently.

6.2 Literature review

6.2.1 The language of crisis

It is noted that language changes whenever a crisis arises. The problem provokes and produces new vocabulary in many languages, especially in English. Language as a form of social behaviour is prone to respond to social events and situations in some particular definite ways. Hence, language use is defined in terms of the social context that produces it. In other words, individual and social groups use language forms and patterns that are the most relevant and appropriate to their experiences and socio-political and cultural situations. In times of crisis, language reflects the physical, social realities and events and the language user's effect, and personal judgements in responding to the conditions. Thus, speakers and writers express evaluative and affective stances when communicating their intentions or making propositions in texts (Chiluwa & Ajiboye, 2016).

Although the extent of linguistic development comparable to COVID-19 is unique, it is also inspired by other periods of history to understand how linguistic creativity manifests in times of severe crisis. For example, World War II introduced the word *radar* as an acronym of *ra*dio *d*etection *a*nd ranging, *fubar* (*f*ucked *u*p *b*eyond *a*ll *r*ecognition), and *snafu* (*s*tatus *n*ominal: *a*ll *f*ucked *u*p). In Vietnam, the word *clusterfuck* denotes a mishandled or disorganised situation, and *fragging* from the shortening of a fragmentation grenade means the deliberate killing of an unpopular member of one's fighting unit.

The United Kingdom's withdrawal from the European Union gave a colloquially known blend word *Brexit* (*Br*itish + *exit*) and other terms, including *brexiteers, remoaners,* and *regrexit.* In contrast, conversations were subject to new concepts such as *backstops, hard borders,* and *cliff edges.* In major health pandemics, the permanent impact on language is usually the names of the diseases registered by the World Health Organization (WHO), such as *H*uman *I*mmunodeficiency *V*irus (HIV), *A*cquired *I*mmune *D*eficiency *S*yndrome (AIDS), Spanish Flu (1918–1920), *S*evere *A*cute *R*espiratory *S*yndrome, SARS (2002–2004), Swine Flu (2009), *J*apanese *E*ncephalitis (JE), and many more.

Nevertheless, Coronavirus (COVID-19) has turned the tables and given an impacting public conversation, principally adding new words to the dictionary entries. Many novel words are introduced all the time, but only a few enter the more comprehensive public forum. They are used effectively, as can be seen in Coronavirus terminology. Coroneologisms is the cover term used by Roig–Martin (2020) to refer to the novel words employed in capturing the understanding of the current pandemic. Many of these words are new coinages or existing words with new meanings used more specifically for comprehension and communication during the pandemic. Aside from English, other major languages have also come up with their coroneologisms.

In the German language, the new words include *Öffnungsdiskussionasorgien* (orgies of discussion) to capture the endless debates on reopening. Other German coroneologisms are *Kontaktverfolgung* (contact tracing), *Schutzmaske* (protective mask), and *Coronaspeck* (stress eating amid stay-at-home). In the Spanish language, the speakers use words like *brote* (outbreak), *cuarantena* (quarantine), *covidiota* (covidiot), and *coronaburro* (*burro* "donkey" signifying dumbness). Spanish speakers distinguish *mascara* "full mask" from *mascarilla* (a mask that partially covers the face). There are new Spanish words such as *teletrabajar* (work from home), *videoconferencia* (videoconference), *videollamada* (video call), and *Zoomleaños* (celebration on Zoom) from the workplace. The Italians also have their share of coroneologisms during the pandemic. Among the words, the Italians are using *focoliao* (hotspot), *tampone* (swab test), *congiunti* (relatives), *denunciari* (to report), *lamentarsi* (to complain), *covidiota* (covidiot), and *untore* (spreader). The Italian word *decreto* (decree) is shortened form of the entire phrase *decreto emergenza* (emergency decree). The Italians still have a positive perspective on life, *andra auto bene*, which translates to all will be fine.

Malachi stated he rarely heard words and phrases related to the pandemic in the Malaysian context before the outbreak (The Star, 2020). Today, however, it is rare to read a newspaper or news website without seeing them. New words have taken on heavier significance, conjuring up all kinds of images whenever someone uses them. As the pandemic grips the world, it can sometimes be easy to get lost in all the new terminology used and bombarded with many new words. Malachi adds that many words were taking on new meanings. The public is now subjected to these words, which we used in the media and various messages circulated.

6.2.2 Word-formation processes

According to Rizki and Marlina (2018), word-formation combines one morpheme with another or modifies its base form. The formation of new words is occasionally compared with semantic modification, which changes its meaning. The word-formation process is a way to develop novel words from continuing components. The important word-formation processes are acronym, abbreviation, back-formation, blending, borrowing, clipping, and folk etymology (Ratih & Gusdian, 2018). The word-formation process creates novel words based on some rules (Yule, 2017). The word-formation process is a way to coin novel words from the existing words based on morphological rules; it can be productive (apt to generate new components) and non-productive (not applicable in forming words). Productivity is a property of word-formation processes of a language; it's one that the language uses a lot and to create new words. Therefore, the productive word-formation processes are used to coin new words in a language. Some of those new words are formed by affixation, compounding, and derivation, which are more prolific, and some by less productive processes (Anderson, 2018). The study uses Yule's (2017, p. 166–185) framework to analyse the word-formation process (Table 6.1).

6.3 Methodology

This study is descriptive qualitative because it presents the data by describing word-formation processes in coining novel words and their meanings. Additionally, the qualitative research design was chosen because it aims to identify word-formation processes and the meanings of the novel words. The researchers used the Oxford English Dictionary (OED, 2020), Dewan Bahasa dan Pustaka (DBP), and The Star newspaper (also online) as the study instruments. The dictionaries

Table 6.1 The word-formation processes

Word-formation processes	Descriptions	Examples
Acronym	A word formed from the initial letters	*CD* (*c*ompact *d*isk) or *VCR* (*v*ideo*c*assette *r*ecorder), where the pronunciation consists of saying each separate letter.
Back-formation	Reduction process (a noun is reduced to another kind, usually a verb)	*television* (n) first came into use, and then *televise* (v) was created. Similarly, *donate* (donation), *emote* (emotion), *enthuse* (enthusiasm), *liaise* (liaison)
Blending	Combination of two detached forms to produce a single word	*smog* ← *sm*oke + *fog*, *brunch* ← *br*eakfast + l*unch*) (typically formed by taking only the beginning of one word and joining it to the end of the other word)
Borrowing	Words are taken from other languages	*croissant* (French), *dope* (Dutch), *lilac* (Persian), *piano* (Italian), *pretzel* (German), *sofa* (Arabic), *tattoo* (Tahitian), *tycoon* (Japanese), and yogurt (Turkish)
Clipping	Occurs when a word of more than one syllable is a shortened form	fax (facsimile), *ad* (advertisement), *bra* (brassiere), *cab* (cabriolet), *condo* (condominium), *flu* (influenza), *pub* (public house), and phone (telephone)
Compounding	The linking of two separate words to produce a single form	**a Nouns** *bookcase, doorknob, fingerprint*, and *sunburn* **b Adjectives** *good-looking, low-paid*, **adjective** + noun (e.g. *fast food*) **c Verbs** *sky-dive, freeze-dry*, adjective + **verb** (e.g. *soft-land*) **d Adverbs** added with *-ly* Compounding is a very productive source of creating a new word.
Conversion	A change in the function of a word, when a noun used as a verb	A noun bottle has come to be used through conversion as a verb e.g. *We bottled the home-brew last night.*

(*Continued*)

Table 6.1 The word-formation processes (*Continued*)

Word-formation processes	Descriptions	Examples
Coinage	The invention of a new term	*aspirin, nylon, vaseline, zipper, granola, Kleenex, Teflon, Xerox, and Google* Google is referring to surfing the Internet to find information.
Derivation	Generally added with affixes	**Prefixes**: *un-* (unhappy), *pre-* (prejudge) **Suffixes:** *-ful* (joyful), *-less* (careless), *-ish* (boyish), *-ism* (terrorism) and *-ness* (sadness) All English words formed by this derivational process have either prefix (*un-,* and *pre-*) or suffix (*-ful,* and *-ish*), or both.
Multiple processes	More than one process at work in the creation of a particular word	*deli* (delicatessen) is borrowed from German and reduces the form

Source: Modified from Yule (2017).

were used to check on the word entries in the respective language. The Star is the most read English newspaper, an online news site, and the most widely read English language newspaper in Malaysia (The Star, 2019). The data collection process took place from December 2019 to October 2020. The selective list of novel words coined in the Malaysian press during the outbreak was gathered and analysed – the researchers chose the samples based on the language used during the outbreak. For example, lists of words used in the newspaper were referred to the dictionaries for further analysis. The types of word-formations were catalogued together with their meanings. The tabulation made the data analysis process organised and produced a general conclusion using Yule's (2017) framework. The processes are divided into three stages: identification, categorisation, and analysis of novel words, as shown in Figure 6.1. The flowchart shows the stages of the data analysis procedure. In stage 1, the researchers identify novel words during the outbreak using OED, DBP, and The Star newspapers. Then, record novel words according to their types and the definitions regarding the language use in the Malaysian context. Finally, the researchers analyse the morphological processing using Yule's (2017) framework.

Stage 1: Identification of Novel Words	Stage 2: Categorisation of Novel Words	Stage 3: Analysis of the Morphological Processes
• Researchers identified newly coined words during the outbreak using OED, DBP and The Star newspapers.	• The newly coined terms/words were recorded according to its types along with definitions based on the language use in the Malaysian context.	• Researchers analysed the morphological processes involved in the creation of the new words using a framework (Yule, 2017).

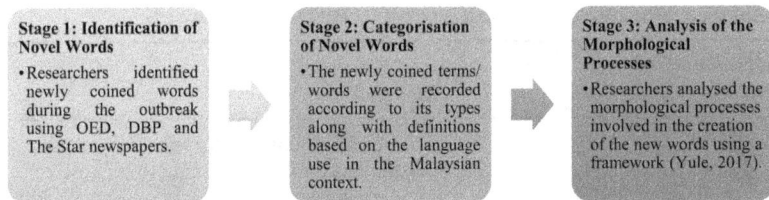

Figure 6.1 The flowchart of data collection and analysis processes of novel word-formation during COVID-19 in Malaysia.

6.4 Findings

The word-formation process plays a vital role in creating new words because coinage aids in creating forms and new words. It can discover and promote the word form of a language and the creation of new words. In the social and cultural context, the new words also highlight current and modern perspectives. Coinage of new words is an essential tool for studying language variation or change. Linguists usually coin innovative words to explain or describe new ideas and things. The word-formation processes such as acronyms, abbreviations, blending, compounding, conversion, initialism, and multiple processes are discussed in this section. Coinage is defined as newly generated words or vocabulary items that are converted into the process of living together. People all over the world use different words to highlight their language effectively during the coronavirus outbreak. This study explored and analysed terms and new words from the perspective of the COVID-19 outbreak (see Table 6.2).

Many governments and other countries accept WHO's terminologies to describe the pandemic. Although many new words were created during the outbreak, Malaysia took some familiar ones from the media and newspapers for use in its vocabulary. The usage and coinage of new words in the Malay language are essential in keeping a language alive. As MCO is adopted, "PKP" (*P*erintah *K*urung *P*ergerakan) gets registered in DBP. More commonly, lexicographers have noticed an exponential increase in the use of a single word and been outmoded as the dominant player in a short time. Communicating the widespread virus to the world has also altered many people's lives, creating new concepts from the fields of epidemiology and medicine, such as pandemic and quarantine, and acronyms, new words to include new social challenges such as isolation and distancing. The consistency of significant social change is closely associated with a substantial lexicographical change in the current crisis.

Table 6.2 Word-formation processes of COVID-19 novel words

Morphological Processes	Novel words	Meaning
ACRONYM	*COVID-19*(Corona Virus Disease 20*19*)	various RNA-containing spherical viruses of the family *Coronaviridae* that cause acute respiratory illnesses
	MCO	Movement Control Order
	CMCO	Conditional Movement Control Order
	RMCO	Recovery Movement Control Order
	EMCO	Enhanced Movement Control Order
	TEMCO	Targeted Enhanced Movement Control Order
	AEMCO	Advance Enhanced Movement Control Order
	PUI	People Under Investigation
	PUS	People Under Surveillance
	PPE	Personal Protective Equipment
	PPV (Pusat Pemberian Vaksin)	vaccination centre
	WFH	Work From Home
	3S (sesak, sempit, sembang)	"*elak* **sesak**" – avoid *crowded* places, "*elak tempat* **sempit**" – avoid *confined* space, "*elak* **sembang** jarak dekat*" – avoid *close* contact
BLEND	*blursday* (**blurs** + every **day**)	every day were passing by in a blur
	coronapalatau (**Corona**virus + ke**pala** + **tahu**)	people who see themselves as subject matter experts despite having shallow knowledge of the subject
	China virus (**China** + Corona**virus**)	referring to Coronavirus, which originated from China
	Chinese virus (**Chinese** + Corona**virus**)	
	covidiot (cov**id** + **id**iot)	a person who stubbornly ignores social distancing protocol, thus helping to spread COVID-19 further
	coronacut (**Corona**virus + **cut**)	haircut post quarantine
	D614G (amino acid, **D** to **G** + position **614**)	mutation in COVID-19 – changes the amino acid at position 614, from D (aspartic acid) to G (glycine)

(*Continued*)

Table 6.2 Word-formation processes of COVID-19 novel words (*Continued*)

Morphological Processes	Novel words	Meaning
	infodemic (*info*rmation + pan*demic*)	quick spreading of both correct and false information about a disease
	Kung-flu (*Kung*fu + *flu*)	referring to Coronavirus, which originated from China
	plandemic (*plan* + pan*demic*)	activities to plan during the quarantine
	SElangkah (*Se*langor + *langkah*)	public health initiative platform to ensure the health and safety of the community to run the business
	zoombombing (*zoom* + photo*bombing*)	unwanted, disruptive intrusion, generally by Internet trolls and hackers, into a video conference call
COMPOUND	*community spread*	refers to people in the same location contracting the virus without a prominent chain of events
	close contact	any individual within 6 feet of an infected person for a total of 15 minutes or more
	Dracula cough	proper way to cough to stop the spread of germs – cough or sneeze into the elbow
	endemic	an infectious disease that spreads quickly among the people of a particular area at the same time
	epidemic	a disease that exists in a particular area for some time
	pandemic	global outbreak
	index case	the first documented case of an infectious disease
	index patient	the first person infected with a disease in an epidemic
	lockdown	individuals are restricted from certain areas in an attempt to control the transmission of disease
	MySejahtera	an app to sign in before entering business premises
	Sivagangga cluster	a cluster has spread out in Kedah, and the spreader got infected from hometown Sivagangga, Tamil Nadu
	super-spreading	a person infected with a virus and spread it to a huge number of individuals
	social distancing	measures that reduce contact between large groups of people
	self-quarantine	strict self-isolation to prevent the spread of disease
	zoonotic	any disease of animals communicable to humans

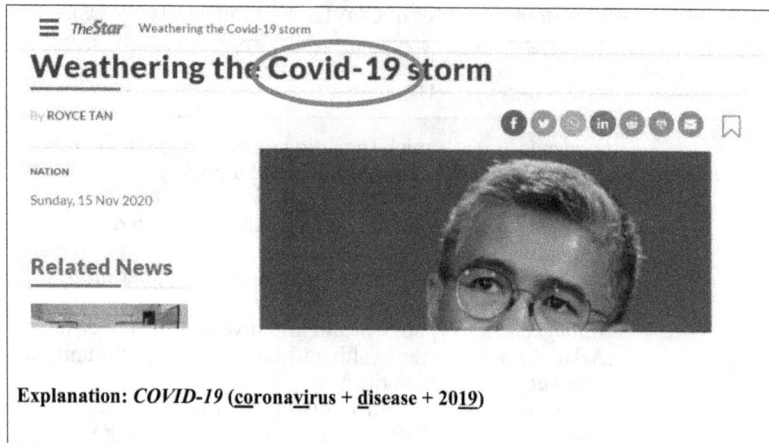

Explanation: *COVID-19* (<u>co</u>rona<u>vi</u>rus + <u>d</u>isease + 20<u>19</u>)

Figure 6.2 Novel word formation through acronym during COVID-19.

6.5 Discussion

6.5.1 Acronym

Based on the analysis, *Co*rona *Vi*rus *D*isease 20*19* (*COVID-19*) refers to any of the various RNA – containing spherical viruses that cause acute respiratory illnesses (Figure 6.2). *COVID-19* is a highly infectious respiratory disease caused by a novel coronavirus. *COVID-19* is universally stated as Coronavirus or Corona that undergoes the morphological process of back clipping. *COVID-19* is denoted as the novel Coronavirus because it is a new virus, which was not discovered previously. Coronaviruses seem to be encircled by a spiky array thought to look like a corona or a crown-like form under a microscope; subsequently, the name is a *coronavirus*. The disease originated from Wuhan, China, in December 2019, called Coronavirus Disease 2019. *COVID-19* is a short form for coronavirus disease and is pronounced as a word. The government has announced a nationwide MCO (*M*ovement *C*ontrol *O*rder) on 18th March 2020 to flatten the curve of COVID-19 infection. Since then, a series of MCO have been implemented depending on conditions within the country (Table 6.2). Taking 3C as an inspiration, in Malaysia (Bernama, 2020), we use 3S ("*elak sesak*" – avoid *crowded* places, "*elak tempat sempit*" – avoid *confined* space, "*elak sembang jarak dekat*" – avoid *close* contact). The term 3S is not pronounced as a word but pronounced by letter.

Acronyms combine the initial letters of a word or phrase; unlike an initialism such as UM (*U*niversiti *M*alaya), an acronym is pronounced phonetically, making them particularly pervasive relatively straight-forward acronyms to become deep-rooted in our lexicon as a stand-alone word.

6.5.2 Blending

Then, *covidiot* (*covid* + *idiot*) is a phonological and graphic blend word, which means overlap by sound and letter without shortening. *Covidiot* means a stupid person who stubbornly ignores social distancing pro-tocol, thus further spreading COVID-19. *D614G* is an alphanumeric blend, which is a combination of alphabets and numbers. Coronavirus is made of spike protein, and the recently discovered mutant of this virus is called D614. The meaning of D614G is the changes in the amino acid at position 614, from D (aspartic acid) to G (glycine). The D614G mutation was first discovered in Europe in February 2020. Recently reported in Malaysia, this mutant strain is ten times more infectious than Coronavirus. There are also some of the regional blends coined during the pandemic in different countries. For example, Donald Trump, ex-United States President, named COVID-19 as *China virus* (*China* + Corona*virus*), *Chinese virus* (*Chinese* + Corona*virus*), and *Kung-flu* (*Kung*fu + *flu*). *China virus* and *Chinese virus* are categorised as phonological overlapped blends. The first source words (China and Chinese) refer to Coronavirus, which originated from China. Similarly, *Kung-flu*, a well-known martial art (Kungfu) from China, overlapped phonologically with the sound of/fu/and flu/flu:/. Another blend of English and Malay languages, *Coronapalatau* (*Corona*virus + ke*pala* + *tahu*), denotes people who suddenly see themselves as subject experts despite not knowing the subject (Figure 6.3). Many people engaged in a virtual meeting, learning, and teaching during the pandemic. *Zoombombing* (*zoom* + photo*bombing*) is a non-overlapping blend, which means unwanted, disruptive intrusion, generally by Internet trolls and hackers, into a video conference call.

6.5.3 Compounding

The terms endemic, epidemic, and pandemic are noun compounds. These are closed compounds because there is no space or hyphen between the words. These compounds consist of a prefix and a free morpheme. The prefixes such as *en-*, *epi-*, and *pan-* were combined with the morpheme demic (Figure 6.4).

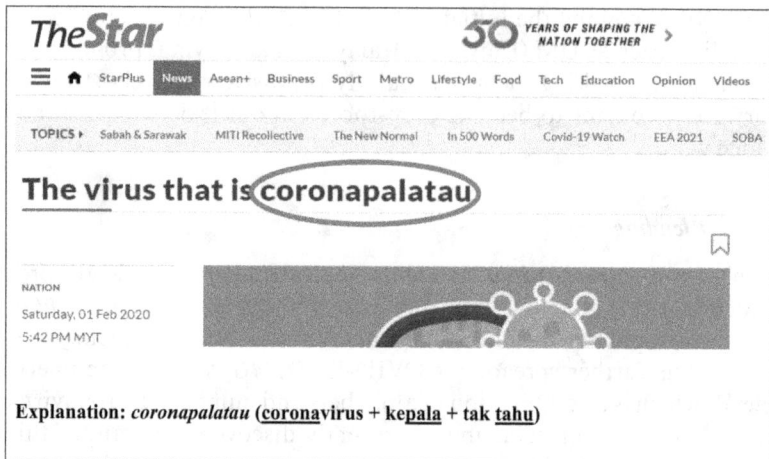

Figure 6.3 Novel word formation through blending during COVID-19.

A prefix is an affix placed before the root word; adding a prefix to the beginning of one word changes it into another word. Each prefix denotes different meanings that occur in loanwords from Greek; *en-* (within, in), *epi-* (upon, over), and *pan-* (all, of everything). The morpheme

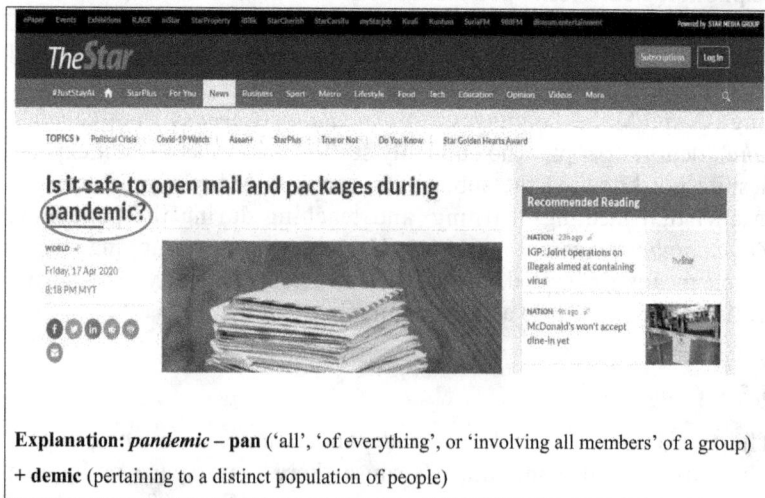

Figure 6.4 Novel word formation through compounding during COVID-19.

demic is an adjective of a distinct population of people. An *endemic* is an infectious disease that spreads quickly among the people of a particular area at the same time. An *epidemic* is an outbreak over a more significant geographical location. When people outside of the Wuhan region began to be infected with COVID-19, the widespread cases of COVID-19 across China meant that the outbreak had grown to an epidemic. WHO declared COVID-19 as a *pandemic* as soon as the outbreak spreads to other regions worldwide.

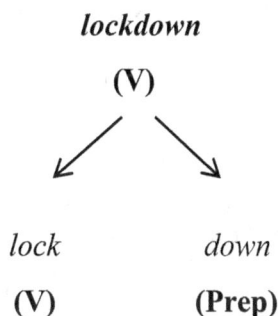

lockdown

(V)

lock   *down*

(V)   **(Prep)**

Lockdown is a **closed compound** word that consists of two free morphemes (lock + down). This **verb compound** is formed of a verb followed by a preposition. *Lockdown* is an emergency measure in which individuals are controlled to go out, and individuals are encouraged to stay home. Lockdown is a phrasal verb because the word "*lock*" acts as a verb. The word "lockdown" has become one of the most familiar terms during the new coronavirus outbreak.

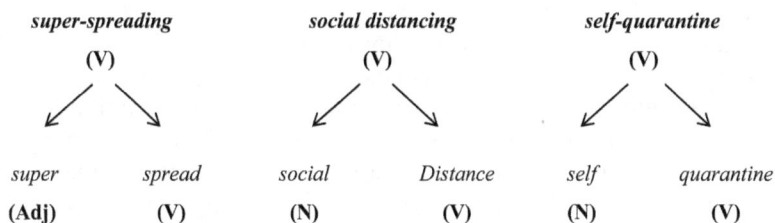

super-spreading		*social distancing*		*self-quarantine*	
(V)		**(V)**		**(V)**	
super	*spread*	*social*	*Distance*	*self*	*quarantine*
(Adj)	**(V)**	**(N)**	**(V)**	**(N)**	**(V)**

The examples mentioned above are compounds. *Super-spreading* and *self-quarantine* are hyphenated compounds because the hyphen (-) separates the words, while *social distancing* is an open compound because there is a space between words. These are **verb compounds** consisting of three morphemes; they are noun, verb, and adjective. The suffix *-ing* is bounded in spread and distance. In super-spreading and social distancing, there are two free morphemes, such as super (Adj) + spread (V) and social (N) + distance (V), which can be independent. The root words spread and distance are added with *-ing*, a bound morpheme that cannot stand alone.

There are two free morphemes in *self-quarantine,* such as self (N) and quarantine (V), forming a verb compound. *Social distancing* refers to measures that reduce contact between big groups of people, such as big gatherings controlling mass travel and working from home. A *super-spreader* is a person who is infected with a virus that produces disease and spreads it to a massive number of individuals who are not infected; COVID-19 is a *super-spreading* event due to its blowout globally. *Self-quarantine* is a strict self-isolation imposed to prevent the spread of disease. *Zoonotic* is related to any disease of animals contagious to humans. The noun form is a zoonosis. The source of COVID-19 is believed to be an animal, a bat, that makes it a zoonotic disease. In zoonotic, the Greek-based English suffix *-sis* (as in words thesis, crisis, basis, paralysis, and analysis) has been added; the plural of this word is formed by replacing the *-sis* with *-ses* (zoonoses). The grapheme/s/changes to/t/in the adjective (zoonotic), another common occurrence, as seen in analysis – analytic, paralysis – paralytic, and so on. The *Tabligh cluster* extended many other subgroups of the cluster respectively based on the place infected with a virus and spread it to many individuals.

6.6 Conclusion

Coroneologisms have shown the rise of many new lexical formations. More than 1,000 new words in both non-specialised and technical terminology have been coined (Thorne, 2020) during the pandemic. Based on the analysis, it can be concluded that novel words are coined by using multiple word-formation processes, which are affixation (prefix, suffix), compounding, abbreviation, acronyms, loan words, blending, clipping. Furthermore, the researchers found interesting findings such as double word-formation processes in creating new words such as clipping + acronym and acronym + blending. The most productive process of coining new words is compounding (Anderson, 2018). The study of word-formation becomes highly productive since it involves morphological processes that are regularly used to produce novel words in a language. Morphology is a combination of elements that are the smallest units of meaning. The English language is growing faster than ever, leaving the older generation lost in the flood of novel words. This fast evolution is taking place in the massive use of mass media and technology. Notably, new lexical items have appeared in many other branches, such as journalism and politics. People are surprisingly creative in coining new expressions to suit their needs and situations.

This chapter presents compounding as the most popular way of coining novel English words during this COVID-19 outbreak. However, multiple processes appear to be quite common depending on the purpose the word has been designed, which defines the most convenient ways. Sometimes a coinage can be by chance that has become popular and accepted in everyday use. There were hundreds of words coined during the pandemic globally (e.g., *Coronacoaster*); however, this study omitted those words concentrating on the terms used in the Malaysian context. This study notices some newly coined words in a category called eponym (e.g., *China virus* and *Chinese virus*). An eponym is a new word based on the name of a person or a place.

These matters will be a spark for future study. This chapter aims to create awareness, educate the public, and record the new words used during the pandemic in the Malaysian context. Besides enriching the corpus terminologies, these terms are essential to give understanding to the community about the dangers of coronavirus infection and measures to prevent or control the spread of the virus (Kasdan et al., 2020). Malachi records some of the common words during the pandemic to create awareness, educate, and present these words to connect with the public (The Star, 2020).

Post-COVID realities and possibilities

As of the time of writing, there are available vaccines in the market such as *Pfizer, Moderna, Johnsons & Johnsons* of the United States, *Oxford-AstraZeneca* of the United Kingdom, *Sinovac* of China, and *Covaxin, Covishield* of India. These vaccines signal the possibility of becoming safe from the COVID-19, the existence of herd immunity, and the imminent return to normalcy. These vaccine names and their trade names will be part of the unique vocabulary that deals with the current pandemic. Moreover, the coroneologisms will form part of any languages' dictionaries since the pandemic affects every linguistic community globally. In the Malaysian context, the new terms such as MySejahtera and SElangkah are inseparable in daily routine.

References

Anderson, C. (2018). Essentials of Linguistic. *Open Textbook Library.* BCcampus Pressbook. Available at: https://essentialsoflinguistics.pressbooks. com (Accessed: 30 March 2020).

Akut, K. B. (2020). Morphological Analysis of the Neologism during the COVID-19 Pandemic. *International Journal of English Language Studies,* *2*(3), 01–07. Available at: https://al-kindipublisher.com/index.php/ijels/article/view/90 (Accessed: 13 December 2020).

Asif, M., Zhiyong, D., Iram, A. & Nisar, M. (2020). Linguistic Analysis of Neologism Related to Coronavirus (COVID-19). *Social Sciences & Humanities Open.* Available at: https://papers.ssrn.com/sol3/papers.cfm (Accessed: 18 December 2020).

Bernama. (2020). Pandemik COVID-19 dan kebergantungan kepada media. Available at: https://www.bernama.com/bm/tintaminda/news.php?id=1851891 (Accessed: 20 April 2021).

Chiluwa, I. & Ajiboye, E. (2016). *Language Use in Crisis Situations: A Discourse Analysis of Online Reactions to Digital News Reports of the Washington Navy Yard Shooting and the Nairobi Westgate Attack.* Nova Science Publishers, Inc. Available at: http://eprints.covenantuniversity.edu.ng/ (Accessed: 4 April 2020).

Harian B. (2021). Available at: https://www.beritaharian.sg/bahasa-budaya/suntikan-istilah-baru-dalam-bahasa-melayu (Accessed: 20 April 2021).

Kasdan, J., Baharudin, R., & Shansuri, A. S. (2020). COVID-19 dalam Korpus Peristilahan Bahasa Melayu: Analisis Sosioterminologi. *GEMA Online® Journal of Language Studies,* *20*(3), 221–241. Available at: http://dx.doi. org/10.17576/gema-2020-2003-13 (Accessed: 30 November 2020).

Luthfiyati, D., Kholiq, A., & Zahroh, I. N. (2017). The Analysis of Word Formation Processes in The Jakarta Post Website. *Journal of Linguistics, English Education and Art (LEEA),* *1*(1). Available at: https://doi.org/10.31539/leea.v1i1.30 (Accessed: 16 June 2020).

Oxford English Dictionary. (2020). Available at: https://public.oed.com/updates/ (Accessed: August 2020).

Piller, I., Zhang, J., & Li, J. (2020). Linguistic Diversity in a Time of Crisis: Language Challenges of the COVID-19 Pandemic. *Multilingual,* *39*(5). Available at: https://www.degruyter.com/document/ (Accessed: 30 October 2020).

Ratih, E. & Gusdian, R. I. (2018). Word Formation Processes in English New Words of Oxford English Dictionary (OED) Online. *Celtic A Journal of Culture English Language Teaching Literature & Linguistic* 5(2), 24. Available at: https://ejournal.umm.ac.id/ (Accessed: 20 May 2020).

Rizki, S. & Marlina, L. (2018). Word Formation Process in Novel Alice's Adventures in Wonderland by Lewis Carroll and Movie Alice in Wonderland by Walt Disney. *e-Journal English Language and Literature,* *7*(1). Available at: http://ejournal.unp.ac.id/ (Accessed: 4 April 2020).

Roig–Marín, A. (2020) English-based Coroneologisms: A Short Survey of Our Covid-19-Related Vocabulary. *English Today*, 1–3. Cambridge University Press. Available at: https://www.cambridge.org/core/journals/english-today/article/abs/englishbased-coroneologisms/ (Accessed: 18 December 2020).

The Star. (2019). Available at: https://www.thestar.com.my/news/nation/2019/09/14/ (Accessed: 30 March 2020).

The Star. (2020). Available at: https://www.thestar.com.my/lifestyle/culture/2020/03/29/malaysian-author-creates-a-user-friendly-covid-19-lexicon (Accessed: 19 May 2020).

Thorne, T. (2020). *CORONASPEAK – The Language of Covid-19 Goes Viral.* King's College London.

Yule, G. (2017). *The Study of Language.* Six Edition. New York: Cambridge University Press. Available at: https://shahroodut.ac.ir (Accessed: 20 June 2020)

Part C
Flattening the curve
Matters on health literacy

7 Public knowledge and perception of COVID-19 and its preventive measures

Edmund Ui-Hang Sim and Su-Hie Ting

7.1 Introduction

Knowledge from research on the transmission route of SARS-CoV-2 is the backbone for recommendation by World Health Organization (WHO) on the lockdown and standard operating procedures (SOPs) for prevention. At the start of the pandemic, the transmission mode of SARS-Cov-2 was suggested to be from droplet that is discharged from a distance of up to 1.8 metres (6 ft) when an infected person following coughs and/or sneezes (CDC, 2020b; La Rosa et al., 2020). Possible transmission routes include speaking (Anfinrud et al., 2020; Stadnytskyi et al., 2020), airborne aerosols (Lewis, 2020), contaminated surfaces (van Doremalen et al., 2020), and stool (Holshue et al., 2020). Nevertheless, all coronaviruses can be destabilised by soap (Gibbens, 2020). The three most important SOPs are physical distancing, wearing of face masks when in public, and avoiding crowded and confined spaces. Azlan et al. (2020) found that Malaysians had low adherence to preventive measures and feared testing (Yau et al., 2020) although they professed good knowledge of COVID-19. The factors that influence perceived effectiveness of COVID-19 preventive measures and adoption of these measures are still not well understood.

This chapter reports the results of a study on health literacy among Malaysians on COVID-19 pandemic, in particular perceived knowledge of COVID-19 disease and effectiveness of preventive measures.

7.2 Literature review

Nomenclature or proper labelling of COVID-19 with respect to the pathogen and disease is often confusing to the layman. When the novel coronavirus was initially identified, it was given a provisional

DOI: 10.4324/9781003182733-10

name of 2019 novel coronavirus (2019-nCoV) (National Center for Immunization and Respiratory Diseases [NCIRD], 2020). Subsequently, it was named Severe Acute Respiratory Syndrome Coronavirus 2 (SARS-CoV-2) (Gorbalenya et al., 2020). This highly contagious SARS-CoV-2 is a single-stranded RNA virus (Chen et al., 2020) and is a successor to the SARS-CoV-1 strain responsible for the 2002–2004 SARS outbreak (van Doremalen et al., 2020). The coronavirus disease that is caused by SARS-CoV-2 is called Coronavirus Disease 2019, and abbreviated as COVID-19 (WHO, 2020a).

In communicating the COVID-19 pandemic, relatively low literacy in the labels for the disease and virus is evident, even among newscasters in international news network channels. Take the example of the common cold, a medical condition affecting those who are sickened by viral infection (rhinoviruses being the most common type). One should not say that they are infected by common cold but by the associated viruses. Only pathogens (viruses, bacteria, and other parasites) can infect people and make them sick. Till now, clinical manifestation of COVID-19 is being studied (Chen et al., 2020; Guan et al., 2020; Huang et al., 2020; Wang et al., 2020; Xu et al., 2020) and variants of the virus have emerged.

Mere knowledge of signs and symptoms of COVID-19 may not create sufficient fear of the severity of the disease if the public are not aware of end-stage complications. Signs and symptoms are generally non-specific (fever, dry cough). Severe conditions are breathing difficulty, persistent chest pain, pneumonia, acute respiratory distress syndrome, sepsis, septic shock, and kidney failure. Other troubling manifestations of COVID-19 can be in the form of thrombotic complications (such as heart attack and stroke) due to deep vein thrombosis (blood clot forming in deep veins) due to arterial blockage in the lungs (Bangalore et al., 2020; Li et al., 2020; Magro et al., 2020). Existing literature reveals that 10%–20% of symptomatic patients can be sick for more than a month (Maxwell, 2020) and the period ranged from two to eight weeks from onset to death (WHO, 2020b). Whilst patients with underlying infirmities that range from cardiovascular disease to cancer are at higher risk of fatality (Wu & McGoogan, 2020), those with hypertension only are not necessarily more susceptible to severe complications (Chow et al., 2020). In Malaysia, association of hypertension and chronic illnesses with COVID-19 deaths may lead the public to wrongly conclude that healthy people are physiologically resistant to the disease.

Adequate knowledge of COVID-19 also includes being aware that asymptomatic and pre-symptomatic individuals who do not show COVID-19 symptoms may still carry the virus and spread the disease (Bai et al., 2020; Kim et al., 2020; Kimball et al., 2020; Mizumoto et al., 2020; Oran & Topol, 2020; Wei et al., 2020). Pre-symptomatic individuals can transmit the virus between one to three days prior to the appearance of symptoms (Wei et al., 2020). WHO (2020c) explained transmission from asymptomatically-infected persons is less likely to be a major driver of the pandemic but Nikolai et al. (2020) have also refuted this, stressing the need for quarantine of asymptomatic people. The latest modelling by US Centers for Disease Control and Prevention shows that 59% of COVID-19 transmissions start with asymptomatic individuals, and 35% of individuals with infection never develop symptoms (The New York Times Company, 2021).

Accurate knowledge of the incubation period is needed for the public to take quarantine orders seriously. Many health authorities (including Malaysia) set 14 days as the quarantine period because the time from exposure to SARS-CoV-2 till symptom onset (called the incubation period) is about five to six days and can even be up to 14 days (Lauer et al., 2020; Yu et al., 2020). Individuals with mild to moderate conditions remain infectious for seven to 12 days, while severe cases can last two weeks (CDC, 2020a). Reflecting on the local situation of Movement Control Order (MCO) flouters (policy makers included) and the mass demonstrations against lockdown measures in Western countries, literacy on preventive measures is wanting.

7.3 Method

The questionnaire data were from 230 respondents on perceived knowledge of COVID-19 disease and effectiveness of preventive measures. Table 7.1 shows the respondents' demographic characteristics.

The self-constructed questionnaire items using five-point Likert scale (strongly agree-agree-neutral-disagree-strongly disagree) are shown in Tables 7.2 and 7.3. The online questionnaire designed using Google Form was disseminated to contacts via purposive sampling on 1–15 July 2020, during the Recovery MCO period when COVID-19 cases were low. The number of new cases was single digit: one on 1 July 2020, and five on 15 July 2020 (Abdullah, 2020a; 2002b). This time frame is important in the interpretation of the results because there was a spike in cases from October 2020, hitting four-digit figures (5,728 cases on 30 January 2021) and five-digit figures (22,948 cases on 19 August 2021) in 2021.

Table 7.1 Demographic characteristics of respondents (N = 230)

Demographic characteristic		Frequency	Percentage
Gender	Female	158	68.70
	Male	72	31.30
Ethnic background	Malay	75	32.61
	Chinese	94	40.87
	Iban	32	13.91
	Bidayuh	11	4.78
	Indian	6	2.61
	Kadazan-Dusun	5	2.17
	Bajau	5	2.17
	Melanau	2	0.87
Occupation	Student	159	69.13
	Unemployed	6	2.61
	Self-employed	15	6.52
	Salaried employees	50	21.74
Monthly income	No income	147	63.91
	Less than RM4,000	43	18.70
	RM4,000–RM5,999	11	4.78
	RM4,000–RM7,999	14	6.09
	RM8,000–RM9,999	3	1.30
	RM10,000–RM11,999	4	1.74
	RM12,000–RM13,999	0	0
	RM14,000–RM15,999	3	1.30
	RM16,000–RM17,999	0	0
	RM18,000–RM19,999	0	0
	More than RM20,000	5	2.17
Educational background	Primary 6 or lower	2	0.87
	Form 3	2	0.87
	Form 5	4	1.74
	Form 6	57	24.78
	Diploma	22	9.57
	Degree or higher	143	62.17

The questionnaire data were coded, and means and standard deviations were calculated. Subsequently, a correlation test was run to determine if there were relationships between the variables. The effect of demographic variables on COVID-19 knowledge and perceived effectiveness of preventive measures were analysed using t-tests (age, income group) and Chi-Square tests (gender, ethnic group).

Table 7.2 Respondents' knowledge of COVID-19 disease (N = 230)

	Knowledge of COVID-19 disease	Mean	SD
1.	I have been getting a lot of information about the COVID-19 disease from newspapers, TV, and internet sources.	4.74	0.49
2.	I have been getting a lot of information about the COVID-19 disease from people around me (e.g. family and friends).	3.87	1.00
3.	I know a lot about the COVID-19 disease.	3.81	0.75
4.	I keep myself informed of the daily global and national statistics of the COVID-19 pandemic.	4.07	0.95
5.	I know more about the COVID-19 disease than other people (e.g., my family and friends).	3.27	0.86
6.	I understand the medical findings on the COVID-19 disease such as the viral load and its connection to the seriousness of the disease.	3.84	0.89
7.	The COVID-19 disease is too complicated [easy] for me to understand.[*R]	3.52	1.01
	Average	3.87	0.96

Table 7.3 Respondents' perceptions on effectiveness of COVID-19 preventive measures (N = 230)

	Perceptions on effectiveness of COVID-19 preventive measures	Mean	SD
1.	As long as I take the necessary precautions I will be safe from the COVID-19 disease, even if I go out often.	3.92	0.97
	Physical distancing	**4.40**	
2.	I feel that avoiding crowded places (e.g. eating in restaurants/kopitiams, and going to markets) will protect me from getting the COVID-19 disease.	4.66	0.56
3.	I believe that avoiding gatherings (e.g. wedding, funeral, religious and conference events) will protect me from getting the COVID-19 disease.	4.66	0.55
4.	I think that staying at home most of the time, and only going out for essentials (food and medicine) will protect me from the COVID-19 disease.	4.49	0.65
5.	I think that working from home is the best way to keep me safe from getting the COVID-19 disease.	4.39	0.76
6.	I think that social or physical distancing (i.e. standing or sitting at least 1 metre away from others) will keep me safe from the COVID-disease.	4.35	0.77
	Personal hygiene	**4.25**	
7.	When I come back from work or activities outside, I take a shower to stay safe from the COVID-19 disease.	4.64	0.62

(*Continued*)

Table 7.3 Respondents' perceptions on effectiveness of COVID-19 preventive measures (N = 230) *(Continued)*

Perceptions on effectiveness of COVID-19 preventive measures	Mean	SD
8. I believe that wearing face mask all the time when I am outside my house will keep me safe from the COVID-19 disease.	4.49	0.65
9. When I come back from work or activities outside, I wash all my clothes (or soak them in detergent) to stay safe from the COVID-19 disease.	4.44	0.81
10. I feel that keeping myself clean (e.g. taking bath regularly) will keep me safe from the COVID-19 disease.	4.20	0.81
11. I believe that washing my hands with soap many times a day keeps me safe from the COVID-19 disease.	4.15	0.83
12. I believe that rubbing my hands with hand sanitizer many times a day will keep me safe from the COVID-19 disease.	3.90	0.88
13. At the petrol station I believe that wearing a disposal plastic glove when holding the petrol pump will keep me safe from the COVID-19 disease.	3.90	1.09
MCO	**4.22**	
14. I believe that the Movement Restriction Order (MCO) imposed by the government protects me from getting the COVID-19 disease.	4.54	0.72
15. I believe that the relaxing of the MCO now will increase my chance of getting the COVID-19 disease.	4.20	0.81
16. I think that the MCO should be longer (until end of the year 2020) to protect us from the COVID-19 disease.	3.92	1.02
SOPs at public premises	**4.07**	
17. I think it is important for me to write down my name and contact number before entering shops or office buildings as a way to control the spread of the COVID-19 disease.	4.37	0.91
18. Using the MySejahtera apps is important to keep me safe from the COVID-19 disease.	3.94	1.06
19. I think that it is important to check my temperature regularly so that I am know whether I have been infected with the COVID-19 disease.	3.90	0.98
Average	4.04	1.08

7.4 Findings and discussion

In this section, the respondents' perceptions of their knowledge of COVID-19 disease and effectiveness of preventive measures are reported.

7.4.1 Perceived knowledge of COVID-19 disease

More than half of the respondents felt that they could understand the COVID-19 disease (mean score of 3.87 out of 5, Table 7.2). Their main sources of information were newspapers, television, and internet sources. They talked about the COVID-19 disease with their family and friends but were only marginally confident that they knew more about the disease than other people. They might not have searched for less readily accessible materials on the disease such as scientific reports and specialist magazines, but relied on daily Ministry of Health, Malaysia reports. These announcements repeatedly emphasised the number of new cases, recovery, and deaths, as well as symptoms and preventive measures, giving rise to moderate knowledge of COVID-19 among Malaysians. In comparison, there is poor knowledge of COVID-19 symptoms and transmissibility in the United States (Al-Hasan et al., 2020) but accurate knowledge among people in Bangladesh (Ferdous et al., 2020) and Nigeria (Reuben et al., 2020).

7.4.2 Perceived effectiveness of COVID-19 preventive measures

Table 7.3 shows the respondents believed in the effectiveness of COVID-19 preventive measures to keep them safe. Among the four categories of measures, the respondents had more confidence in physical distancing than in personal hygiene, MCO and SOP compliance at public places. Among the recommended measures, the highest efficacy was attributed to avoiding crowded places and avoiding gatherings, and the lowest efficacy to using hand sanitizer and plastic gloves, and performing temperature checks – possibly due to the emphasis on the former in public service announcements.

Finally, although the respondents were also confident in the effectiveness of MCO and SOPs at public premises for contact tracing, these SOPs were considered less effective than personal initiatives (physical distancing and personal hygiene). Perceptions of the low efficacy of MCO and SOPs at public places might explain low compliance with these COVID-19 management guidelines.

7.4.3 Correlation between knowledge of COVID-19 disease and perceived effectiveness of preventive measures

Table 7.4 shows that the only demographic variable that influenced knowledge of COVID-19 was gender. Female and male respondents

Table 7.4 Mean scores showing the effect of demographic variables on knowledge of COVID-19 disease

Demographic variables		Mean score
Gender	Female	3.93*
	Male	3.76*
Ethnic background	Malay	3.82
	Chinese	3.54
	Indian	3.88
	Indigenous	3.85
Educational level	No degree	3.86
	Degree	3.88
Income level	Below RM4,000 (B40)	3.89
	Above RM4,000 (M40 and T20)	3.81

Note: Significant at *p < 0.001

were significantly different in their knowledge of COVID-19 disease (p < 0.001). The female respondents (M = 3.93) had slightly better knowledge of the disease than the male respondents (M = 3.76).

The three demographic variables that might influence perceived effectiveness of COVID-19 preventive measures are gender, educational level, and income level (Table 7.5). Female and male respondents were significantly different in their perceptions of the effectiveness of COVID-19 preventive measures (p < 0.01). Female respondents (M = 4.07) had higher perceived efficacy of recommended measures than male respondents (M = 3.98). The propensity of females to have better

Table 7.5 Mean scores showing the effect of demographic variables on perceived effectiveness of preventive measures

Demographic variables		Mean score
Gender	Female	4.07*
	Male	3.98*
Ethnic background	Malay	4.09
	Chinese	3.98
	Indian	4.25
	Indigenous	4.11
Educational level	No degree	3.99*
	Degree	4.07*
Income level	Below RM4,000 (B40)	4.06*
	Above RM4,000 (M40 and T20)	3.94*

Note: Significant at *p < 0.01

literacy of COVID-19 is linked to their role to care for family which familiarises them with healthcare information and systems (Won & Pascall, 2004).

When the respondents were divided into two groups based on their educational level, the t-test showed that there was a significant difference between the university graduates and those without degrees in their perceptions of the effectiveness of COVID-19 preventive measures (p = 0.008). The mean scores in Table 7.4 show that university graduates (M = 4.07) were more likely to believe in the effectiveness of the preventive measures than respondents without a degree (M = 3.99). In view of this, SOP compliance is likely to be higher among educated individuals.

Similarly, perceived effectiveness of COVID-19 preventive measures was significantly different for respondents with income in the B40 and higher brackets (p < 0.01). Interestingly, respondents in the B40 income bracket (M = 4.06) were more likely to believe in the effectiveness of the COVID-19 measures than those in the higher income bracket (M = 3.94), who may question the efficacy.

7.5 Conclusion

The study showed moderate knowledge of COVID-19 disease, with females having better knowledge. There was strong confidence in the effectiveness of preventive measures among the respondents, particularly among university graduates and the lower socio-economic group. The social determinants of health literacy pertaining to COVID-19 preventive measures seemed to be gender, education, and socio-economic status.

Malaysians seem to have developed COVID-19 health literacy quickly because the present study was conducted in July 2020, half a year after the first Malaysian COVID-19 case on 4 February 2020. The moderate level of perceived literacy on COVID-19 disease could reflect the success of updates by the Ministry of Health and frequent public service announcements. Individuals with good health literacy are more likely to take preventive measures, seek treatment when they fall sick (Scott et al. 2002), or go for COVID-19 screening if they show symptoms or have come into contact with COVID-19 positive individuals. With 70% of COVID-19 cases being asymptomatic in Malaysia (Tang, 2020), health literacy becomes even more crucial because people can unintentionally pass the disease to others. Therefore, to encourage individual and collective action in adopting preventive measures, it is important to frame health messages to bring personal and social benefits to different sectors of the community. Future research should investigate elements of COVID-19 messages which cue health protective action.

Post-COVID realities and possibilities

Post-COVID-19 realities and possibilities related to moderate perceived knowledge of COVID-19 disease and high perceived effectiveness of preventive measures are in the area of social interactions and health. People will get accustomed to less social contact as physical distancing becomes internalised. With constant messages on sanitisation, people develop a better understanding of viruses and bacteria and how to combat public health threats using vaccines. There is likely to be better appreciation of research and government decisions in health issues.

References

Abdullah, N.H., 2020a. *Kenyataan Akhbar KPK 1 Julai 2020 – Situasi Semasa Jangkitan Penyakit Coronavirus 2019 (COVID-19) di Malaysia.* Retrieved from https://kpkesihatan.com/2020/07/01/kenyataan-akhbar-kpk-1-julai-2020-situasi-semasa-jangkitan-penyakit-coronavirus-2019-covid-19-di-malaysia/.

Abdullah, N.H., 2020b. *Kenyataan Akhbar KPK 15 Julai 2020 – Situasi Semasa Jangkitan Penyakit Coronavirus 2019 (COVID-19) di Malaysia.* Retrieved from https://kpkesihatan.com/2020/07/15/kenyataan-akhbar-kpk-15-julai-2020-situasi-semasa-jangkitan-penyakit-coronavirus-2019-covid-19-di-malaysia/.

Al-Hasan, A., Yim, D., & Khuntia, J., 2020. Citizens' adherence to COVID-19 mitigation recommendations by the government: A 3-country comparative evaluation using web-based cross-sectional survey data. *Journal of Medical Internet Research*, *22*(8), Article e20634.

Anfinrud, P., Stadnytskyi, V., Bax, C.E., & Bax, A., 2020. Visualizing speech-generated oral fluid droplets with laser light scattering. *The New England Journal of Medicine*, *382*(21), pp. 2061–2063. Retrieved from https://doi.org/10.1056/NEJMc2007800.

Azlan, A.A., Hamzah, M.R., Sern, T. J., Ayub, S.H., & Mohamad, E., 2020. Public knowledge, attitudes and practices towards COVID-19: A cross-sectional study in Malaysia. *PLOS One*, *15*(5), Article e0233668.

Bai Y., Yao L., Wei T., Tian F., Jin D.Y., Chen L., & Wang M. 2020. Presumed asymptomatic carrier transmission of COVID-19. *JAMA*, *323*(14), 1406–1407. doi: 10.1001/jama.2020.2565. PMID: 32083643; PMCID: PMC7042844.

Bangalore, S., Sharma, A., Slotwiner, A., Yatskar, L., Harari, R., Shah, B., Ibrahim, H., Friedman, G.H., Thompson, C., Alviar, C.L., Chadow,

H.L., Fishman, G.I., Reynolds, H.R., Keller, N., & Hochman, J.S., 2020. ST-segment elevation in patients with COVID-19: A case series. *New England Journal of Medicine*, 382(25), pp. 2478–2480. doi: 10.1056/NEJMc2009020.

Centers for Disease Control and Prevention (CDC), 2020a, October 19. *Coronavirus Disease 2019 (COVID-19): Duration of Isolation and Precautions for Adults with COVID-19*. CDC (U.S. Department of Health & Human Services). Atlanta, Georgia, U.S. Retrieved from https://www.cdc.gov/coronavirus/ 2019-ncov/hcp/duration-isolation.html.

Centers for Disease Control and Prevention (CDC), 2020b, October 5. *Coronavirus Disease 2019 (COVID-19): How COVID-19 Spreads*. CDC (U.S. Department of Health & Human Services). Atlanta, Georgia, U.S. Retrieved from https://www.cdc.gov/coronavirus/2019-ncov/prevent-getting-sick/how-covid-spreads.html?CDC_AA_refVal=https%3A%2F%2Fwww.cdc.gov% 2Fcoronavirus%2F2019-ncov%2Fprepare%2Ftransmission.html.

Chen, N., Zhou, M., Dong, X., Qu, J., Gong, F., Han, Y., ... & Yu, T., 2020. Epidemiological and clinical characteristics of 99 cases of 2019 novel coronavirus pneumonia in Wuhan, China: A descriptive study. *The Lancet*, 395(10223), pp. 507–513.

Chow, N., Fleming-Dutra, K., Gierke, R., Hall, A. Hughes, M., Pilishvili, T., Ritchey, M., Roguski, K., Skoff, T., & Ussery, E., 2020. Preliminary estimates of the prevalence of selected underlying health conditions among patients with Coronavirus Disease 2019 – United States, February 12–March 28, 2020. *MMWR Morbidity and Mortality Weekly Report*, 69(13), pp. 382–386. doi: 10.15585/mmwr.mm6913e2.

Ferdous, M.Z., Islam, M.S., Sikder, M.T., Mosaddek, A.S.M., Zegarra-Valdivia, J.A., & Gozal, D., 2020. Knowledge, attitude, and practice regarding COVID-19 outbreak in Bangladesh: An online-based cross-sectional study. *PLOS One*, 15(10), Article e0239254.

Gibbens, S., 2020, March 18. Why soap is preferable to bleach in the fight against coronavirus. National Geographic. Retrieved from https://www. nationalgeographic.com/science/2020/03/why-soap-preferable-bleach-fight-against-coronavirus/.

Gorbalenya, A.E., Baker, S.C., Baric, R.S., de Groot, R.J., Drosten, C., Gulyaeva, A.A., ... & Penzar, D., 2020. The species severe acute respiratory syndrome related coronavirus: Classifying 2019-nCoV and naming it SARS-CoV-2. *Nature Microbiology*, 5(4), pp. 536–544.

Guan, W.J., Ni, Z.Y., Hu, Y., Liang, W.H., Ou, C.Q., He, J.X., ... & Du, B., 2020. Clinical characteristics of coronavirus disease 2019 in China. *New England Journal of Medicine*, 382(18), pp. 1708–1720.

Holshue, M.L., DeBolt, C., Lindquist, S., Lofy, K.H., Wiesman, J., Bruce, H., Spitters, C., Ericson, K., Wilkerson, S., Tural, A., Diaz, G., Cohn, A., Fox, L., Patel, A., Gerber, S.I., Kim, L., Tong, S., Lu, X., Lindstrom, S., Pallansch, M.A., ... Washington State 2019-nCoV Case Investigation Team, 2020. First case of 2019 novel coronavirus in the United States. *The New England Journal of Medicine*, 382(10), pp. 929–936. Retrieved from https://doi.org/10.1056/ NEJMoa2001191.

Huang, C., Wang, Y., Li, X., Ren, L., Zhao, J., Hu, Y., ... & Cheng, Z., 2020. Clinical features of patients infected with 2019 novel coronavirus in Wuhan, China. *The Lancet, 395*(10223), pp. 497–506.

Kim G.U., Kim, M.J., Ra, S.H., Lee, J., Bae, S., Jung, J., & Kim, S.H., 2020. Clinical characteristics of asymptomatic and symptomatic patients with mild COVID-19. *Clinical Microbiology and Infection, 26*(7), pp. 948.e1–948.e3. doi: 10.1016/j.cmi.2020.04.040.

Kimball, A., Hatfield, K.M., Arons, M., James, A., Taylor, J., Spicer, K., ... & Bell, J.M., 2020. Asymptomatic and presymptomatic SARS-CoV-2 infections in residents of a long-term care skilled nursing facility—King County, Washington. *Morbidity and Mortality Weekly Report, 69*(13), pp. 377–381.

La Rosa, G., Bonadonna, L., Lucentini, L., Kenmoe, S., & Suffredini, E., 2020. Coronavirus in water environments: Occurrence, persistence and concentration methods – A scoping review. *Water Research, 179*, Article 115899. Retrieved from https://doi.org/10.1016/j.watres.2020.115899.

Lauer, S.A., Grantz, K.H., Bi, Q., Jones, F.K., Zheng, Q., Meredith, H.R., ... & Lessler, J., 2020. The incubation period of coronavirus disease 2019 (COVID-19) from publicly reported confirmed cases: Estimation and application. *Annals of Internal Medicine, 172*(9), pp. 577–582.

Lewis, D., 2020. Mounting evidence suggests coronavirus is airborne—but health advice has not caught up. *Nature, 583*(7817), pp. 510–513.

Li, Y., Li, M., Wang, M., Zhou, Y., Chang, J., Xian, Y., Wang, D., Mao, L., Jin, H., & Hu, B., 2020. Acute cerebrovascular disease following COVID-19: A single center, retrospective, observational study. *Stroke and Vascular Neurology, 5*(3), pp. 279–284. doi: 10.1136/svn-2020-000431.

Magro, C., Mulvey, J.J., Berlin, D., Nuovo, G., Salvatore, S., Harp, J., Baxter-Stoltzfus, A., & Laurence, J., 2020. Complement associated microvascular injury and thrombosis in the pathogenesis of severe COVID-19 infection: A report of five cases. *Translation Research, 220*, pp. 1–13. doi: 10.1016/j.trsl.2020.04.007.

Maxwell, E., 2020. Living with COVID-19: A dynamic review of the evidence around ongoing COVID-19 symptoms (often called Long COVID). Retrieved from https://evidence.nihr.ac.uk/wp-content/uploads/2020/10/Living-with-Covid-Themed-Review.pdf.

Mizumoto, K., Kagaya, K., Zarebski, A., & Chowell, G. (2020). Estimating the asymptomatic proportion of coronavirus disease 2019 (COVID-19) cases on board the Diamond Princess cruise ship, Yokohama, Japan. *Eurosurveillance, 25*(10), Article 2000180. doi: 10.2807/1560-7917.

National Center for Immunization and Respiratory Diseases (NCIRD), 2020. *About 2019 Novel Coronavirus (2019-nCoV)*. Centers for Disease Control and Prevention, U.S. Department of Health & Human Services. Atlanta, Georgia. Retrieved from https://www.cdc.gov/coronavirus/2019-ncov/about/index.html.

Nikolai, L.A., Meyer, C.G., Kremsner, P.G., & Velavan, T.P., 2020. Asymptomatic SARS Coronavirus 2 infection: Invisible yet invincible. *International*

Journal of Infectious Diseases, *100*, pp. 112–116. Retrieved from https://doi.org/10.1016/j.ijid.2020.08.076

Oran, D.P., & Topol, E.J., 2020. Prevalence of asymptomatic SARS-CoV-2 infection: A narrative review. *Annals of Internal Medicine*, *173*(5), pp. 362–367. doi: 10.7326/M20-3012.

Reuben, R.C., Danladi, M.M., Saleh, D.A., & Ejembi, P.E., 2020. Knowledge, attitudes and practices towards COVID-19: An epidemiological survey in North-Central Nigeria. *Journal of Community Health*, pp. 1–14. Retrieved from https://doi.org/10.1007/s10900-020-00881-1

Scott, T.L., Gazmararian, J.A., Williams, M.V., & Baker, D.W., 2002. Health literacy and preventive health care use among medicare enrollees in a managed care organization. *Medical Care*, *40*(5), pp. 395–404.

Stadnytskyi, V., Bax, C.E., Bax, A., & Anfinrud, P., 2020. The airborne lifetime of small speech droplets and their potential importance in SARS-CoV-2 transmission. *Proceedings of the National Academy of Sciences of the United States of America*, *117*(22), pp. 11875–11877. Retrieved from https://doi.org/10.1073/pnas.2006874117

Tang, A., 2020, July 8. COVID-19: 70% of cases in Malaysia were asymptomatic, says Health DG. The Star. Retrieved from. https://www.thestar.com.my/news/nation/2020/07/08/covid-19-70-of-cases-in-malaysia-were-asymptomatic-says-health-dg.

The New York Times Company, 2021, January 13. *CDC analysis: More than half of all COVID-19 transmission begins with people that show no symptoms.* Retrieved from https://www.firstpost.com/tech/science/cdc-analysis-shows-over-half-of-all-covid-19-transmission-begins-with-people-that-show-no-symptoms-9196861.html.

The Star, 2020, October 12. Conditional MCO: Dos and don'ts for Sabah, Selangor and others. Retrieved from https://www.thestar.com.my/news/nation/2020/10/12/conditional-mco-dos-and-don039ts-for-sabah-selangor-and-others.

Van Doremalen, N., Bushmaker, T., Morris, D.H., Holbrook, M.G., Gamble, A., Williamson, B.N., ... & Lloyd-Smith, J.O., 2020. Aerosol and surface stability of SARS-CoV-2 as compared with SARS-CoV-1. *New England Journal of Medicine*, *382*(16), pp. 1564–1567. Retrieved from https://doi.org/10.1056/NEJMc2004973.

Wang, D., Hu, B., Hu, C., Zhu, F., Liu, X., Zhang, J., ... & Zhao, Y., 2020. Clinical characteristics of 138 hospitalized patients with 2019 novel coronavirus–infected pneumonia in Wuhan, China. *JAMA*, *323*(11), pp. 1061–1069.

Wei, W.E., Li, Z., Chiew, C.J., Yong, S.E., Toh, M.P., & Lee, V.J., 2020. Presymptomatic Transmission of SARS-CoV-2—Singapore, January 23–March 16, 2020. *Morbidity and Mortality Weekly Report*, *69*(14), pp. 411–415.

Won S-Y. & Pascall, G., 2004. A Confucian war over childcare? Practice and policy in childcare and their implications for understanding the Korean gender regime. *Social Policy & Administration*, *38*(3), pp. 270–829. doi: 10.1111/j.1467-9515.2004.00390.x.

World Health Organization (WHO), 2020a. Naming the coronavirus disease (COVID-19) and the virus that causes it. Retrieved from https://www.who.int/emergencies/diseases/novel-coronavirus-2019/technical-guidance/naming-the-coronavirus-disease-(covid-2019)-and-the-virus-that-causes-it.

World Health Organization (WHO), 2020b. Report of the WHO-China Joint Mission on Coronavirus Disease 2019 (COVID-19). Retrieved from https://www.who.int/publications/i/item/report-of-the-who-china-joint-mission-on-coronavirus-disease-2019-(covid-19).

World Health Organization (WHO), 2020c. Transmission of COVID-19 by asymptomatic cases. Retrieved from http://www.emro.who.int/health-topics/corona-virus/transmission-of-covid-19-by-asymptomatic-cases.html.

Wu, Z., & McGoogan, J. M., (2020). Characteristics of and important lessons from the coronavirus disease 2019 (COVID-19) outbreak in China: summary of a report of 72 314 cases from the Chinese Center for Disease Control and Prevention. *Journal of the American Medical Association (JAMA)*, *323*(13), pp. 1239–1242.

Xu, X.W., Wu, X.X., Jiang, X.G., Xu, K.J., Ying, L.J., Ma, C.L., ... & Sheng, J.F., 2020. Clinical findings in a group of patients infected with the 2019 novel coronavirus (SARS-Cov-2) outside of Wuhan, China: Retrospective case series. *British Medical Journal*, *368*, article m606.

Yau, E.K.B., Pang, N.T.P., Shoesmith, W.D., James, S., Nor Hadi, N.M., & Loo, J.L., 2020. The behaviour changes in response to COVID-19 pandemic within Malaysia. *The Malaysian Journal of Medical Sciences*, *27*(2), pp. 45–50.

Yu, P., Zhu, J., Zhang, Z., & Han, Y., 2020. A familial cluster of infection associated with the 2019 novel coronavirus indicating possible person-to-person transmission during the incubation period. *The Journal of Infectious Diseases*, *221*(11), pp. 1757–1761.

8 Knowledge, attitude, and practice on health and legal measures

Natasya Abdullah, Noor Dzuhaidah Osman, Nur Syazana Umar, Muhammad Nizam Awang, and Zairina A Rahman

8.1 Introduction

The COVID-19 infection, which started in late 2019, has spread globally, reaching into every continent and to date, causing more than 70 million cases and nearly 2 million deaths worldwide. The infection, first detected in Wuhan, China, is caused by the novel coronavirus, severe acute respiratory syndrome coronavirus 2 (SARS-CoV-2), which infects the respiratory tract (WHO, 2020c). Transmission from human to human occurs through respiratory droplets or via contact with the eyes, mouth, and nose (Carlos et al., 2020). Presentation of the symptoms varies from being asymptomatic to a very severe respiratory and multiple organ failure that often leads to death.

There is still no specific treatment for this disease; hence symptomatic treatment remains the primary management, and respiratory support is needed in most cases. The results of a few off-label trials using anti-virals, anti-malarials, and steroids were controversial, and the outcomes remain inconclusive (Kalil, 2020). With a dire situation, our current hope would be to develop the individual self-immune system through vaccination. Some pharmaceutical companies such as Pfizer BionTech and Astra Zeneca's have successfully developed and manufactured the vaccines in most countries. However, it would be too early to tell the effectiveness and safety issues in the near future (Teoh & Basyir, 2021).

With so many uncertainties, public health interventions became a priority to prevent the spread of the virus. The World Health Organisation (WHO) have listed several simple yet effective mitigation activities for the public that include wearing a face mask, physical distancing, maintaining hand hygiene, and avoiding crowded places.

DOI: 10.4324/9781003182733-11

In Malaysia, escalating cases of COVID-19 infection has forced the government to gazette Prevention and Control of Infectious Diseases (Measures within the Infected Local Areas) Regulations 2020 (Regulations) (Aziz et al., 2020). These regulations were enforced in different phases of Movement Control Orders (MCOs) to prevent the control and spread of the COVID-19 pandemic. However, the sudden evident uptrend of cases and the emergence of new clusters raise the question of whether the MCOs have been sufficiently robust and effective.

The public's ability to understand the importance of such measures is paramount in addressing health communication and policies. Understanding the information could lead to the acceptance of the situation and subsequently translate to their reaction in terms of attitude and practices. Therefore, this chapter will provide the results of an online survey of the Malaysian public knowledge, attitude, and practice (KAP) on the health and legal measures. The study was conducted during the 2nd wave of the pandemic from June 2020 to August 2020 using validated questionnaires.

8.1.1 Confronting the pandemic

8.1.1.1 Malaysia's response to COVID-19

Malaysia is one of the countries that responded early to the WHO's pandemic warning as soon as it was detected in China. Based on the guidelines from the WHO and evidence from other countries, the Malaysian government, led by the Ministry of Health, has made several contingency plans and preparations to face the surge of infection. These include training the staff, preparing the diagnostic lab, and designating a few hospitals solely to treat COVID-19 patients (Aziz et al., 2020).

As soon as the second wave of infection took place in late February 2020, the government took a bold decision and initiated the MCO, which extended to two months until May 2020. Subsequently, the country moved to Conditional Movement Control Order (CMCO) before moving to Recovery Movement Control Order (RMCO) a month later (Tang, 2020). During this period, there were firm restrictions of mass group movement except for individuals to obtain essential items such as food and medicines. Almost all socio-economic sectors were closed together with the closure of the country's borders. The education sector was equally affected where higher learning institutions were closed, and students resorted to remote learning.

Although the decision to implement the MCOs was not popular in some communities, it had given a chance, particularly to the health authorities, to screen and isolate positive cases to break the transmission chain (Aziz et al., 2020). As part of the mitigation activities, the public was highly encouraged to be more vigilant and religiously adhere to a combination of strategies. These include the campaign of practising 3Ws (i.e. wearing a face mask in public areas, washing hands, warn others to practice physical distancing) and avoiding 3Cs (closed conversation, confined spaces, and crowded places).

8.1.1.2 Legal measures

The escalating COVID-19 cases in the country has forced the government to gazette the Prevention and Control of Infectious Diseases (PCID) (Measures Within the Infected Local Areas) Regulations 2020 effective 18th March 2020 and were extended to several phases to cover the period of Movement Control Orders (MCOs). The country's administration during the pandemic is under the scrutiny and control of the National Security Council legalised by the National Security Act (NSC) 2016 (Act 776) to provide for policies and strategy measures to oversee, monitor, regulate, and enforce regulations on the current pandemic situation in the country. In addition, the Police Act 1967 (Act 344) provided the power to the police to stop and prevent unnecessary travel such as only for necessity such for work purposes, purchasing of groceries, and other necessities. Under this Act, the Ministry of Health is considered the authorised officer to instruct any appropriate measures necessary to control the disease, including imposing quarantine, mandatory use of the face mask, registration upon entering public places, and preventing any social gathering.

The implementation of the rules, regulations, and laws during the various movement control orders in Malaysia was relatively strict compared to other neighbouring countries such as Indonesia and Thailand. During the implementation of the first phase of the movement control order (MCO), no interstate travels were allowed, and only certain public essentials services such as markets and pharmacies could operate. Later during the second phase of MCO i.e. the CMCO (started 4th May 2020), most economic activities were allowed except for sports and public gatherings. However, interstate travel was not permitted unless in some exceptional circumstances such as for work and emergencies. Afterwards, during RMCO (started 10th June 2020), interstate travel was allowed together with some religious, sports, and holiday activities. These MCO measures seem successful to flatten the COVID-19 curve in Malaysia (Table 8.1).

Table 8.1 Phases of movement control orders implemented in Malaysia and the related laws

Phase/period	The laws in force
Phase 1 18th –31st March 2020	• Prevention and Control of Infectious Diseases (Declaration of Infected Local Areas) Order 2020 • Prevention and Control of Infectious Diseases (Measures within the Infected Local Areas) Regulations 2020 • Prevention and Control of Infectious Diseases (Compounding of Offences) (Amendment) Regulations 2020
Phase 2 1st –14th April 2020	• Prevention and Control of Infectious Diseases (Declaration of Infected Local Areas) (Extension of Operation) Order 2020 • Prevention and Control of Infectious Diseases (Measures within Infected Local Areas) (No.2) Regulations 2020 • Prevention and Control of Infectious Diseases (Measures within Infected Local Areas) (No.2) (Amendment) Regulations 2020 • Prevention and Control of Infectious Diseases (Compounding of Offences) (Amendment) (No. 2) Regulations 2020
Phase 3 15th –28th April 2020	• Prevention and Control of Infectious Diseases (Declaration of Infected Local Areas) (Extension of Operation) Order 2020 • Prevention and Control of Infectious Diseases (Measures within Infected Local Areas) (No.3) Regulations 2020
Phase 4 29th April– 12th May 2020	• Prevention and Control of Infectious Diseases Regulation (Measures within the Infected Local Areas) (No.4) Regulations 2020 (revoked) • Prevention and Control of Infectious Diseases Regulation (Measures within the Infected Local Areas) (No.5) Regulations 2020
Phase 5 13th May–9th June 2020	• Prevention and Control of Infectious Diseases Regulation (Measures within the Infected Local Areas) (No.6) Regulations 2020
Phase 6 10th June– 31st August 2020	• Prevention and Control of Infectious Diseases Regulation (Measures within the Infected Local Areas) (No.7) Regulations 2020
Phase 7 1st September– 31st December 2020	• Prevention and Control of Infectious Diseases Regulation (Measures within the Infected Local Areas) (No.8) Regulations 2020 • Prevention and Control of Diseases of Infectious Diseases (Declaration of Infected Local Areas (Extension of Operation (No.7) Order 2020
Phase 8 1st January– 31st March 2021	• Prevention and Control of Infectious Diseases Regulation (Measures within the Infected Local Areas) (No.9) Regulations 2020

Any deviance from measures under this regulation is punishable with a fine not exceeding RM1,000 or six-months imprisonment or both under the Prevention and Control of Infectious Diseases (Measures within Infected Local Areas) (No. 2) Regulations 2020 ("Phase 2 Regulations"). Subsequent or repeat offences will attract heavier penalties. As the measures successfully flattened the pandemic curve at that time, it can safely be deduced that the strict rules and regulations that adopt the command-and-control strategy could reduce violators and deter the public from disobeying the law in force. Compared with the Swedish government's measures, which was known to have a more relaxed approach, the number of cases was high, reaching more than 500 thousand cases and more than 10,000 deaths (Claeson & Hanson, 2021).

The rules and regulations are designated to control society by ensuring obedience towards health and legal measures. However, despite the health and legal enforcement, society's knowledge, attitude, and practice in realising these measures are essential factors in combating this pandemic. This statement is especially true in unveiling public awareness that can identify knowledge gaps, cultural beliefs, or behavioural patterns that may facilitate understanding and action, as well as pose problems or create barriers to development efforts in this sector.

8.1.1.3 ENSURING EFFECTIVE COMMUNICATION

The pandemic has brought many uncertainties and life changes, leading to anxiety and panic among the public. The situation has forced people to adjust their normal lifestyle and behaviour, which may not be acceptable for some, hence jeopardising any effort to curb the infection. While COVID-19 seems to be the main threat, the emerging infodemic (not clear may be equally harmful as the virus itself (WHO, 2020b). During this time, mass information is shared across the globe at lightning speed and the biggest concern would be sharing false, unverified information and data. History has shown that misinformation towards certain infectious disease posed threats to healthcare providers (Turan et al., 2016) and disrupted the public's health by creating fear and stigma (The Lancet, 2020).

Multiple government and non-governmental agencies work hand-in-hand with the Ministry of Health to manage the country's pandemic. The two prominent agencies are the Crisis Preparedness and Response Centre (CPRC) and the National Security Council, responsible for coordinating, managing, and monitoring the situation related to health and security. To gain public trust and ensure control of the situation, only verified and updated data were shared with the public, which is also crucial to prevent panic and confusion (The Lancet, 2020). Daily briefings were conducted by two official figures, namely the Minister of Defence, on security matters related to the movement control orders (MCOs) and the Director General of Health on any health-related matters.

The authorities' daily briefings were broadcast live on dedicated television and radio channels to ensure extensive and accessible community engagement. With the rampant use of the Internet and technology in this era, information sharing was done through official government websites using multilingual creative visual content in infographics, video, and even cartoons to cater to the young ones. Social media platforms such as *Facebook* and *Twitter* were fully utilised. Likewise, daily messages using mobile's short messaging system (SMS) to every registered number in the country have helped deliver the information to those with limited or no excess to the Internet.

Correcting the public perception was considered imperative as it could influence the public's behaviour and their willingness to adhere to any standard operating procedures (SOP). As the COVID-19 cases increased, so did the number of rumours, fake news, and false claims on effective treatment. Hence, the government has attempted to disseminate messages effectively and strategically while at the same time, implement strict measures against violators of any misconduct. To ensure control of the situation, the Malaysian Communication and Multimedia Commission (MCMC), an agency that regulates the communications and multimedia industry in the country, works closely with the police to monitor and take legal action against anyone spreading false and fabricated information.

8.2 Literature review

8.2.1 *International previous studies on understanding, acceptance, and adherence*

As soon as the pandemic emerged globally, we observed an increasing number of studies related to the understanding, acceptance, and adherence of the public towards various control measures were implemented in their own respective countries. A short-term survey during this time would be helpful to gauge the public health knowledge and practices. At the same time, it would help to collect feedback that can be used for future intervention programs and new health policy-making. It would also be critical for the government and the authorities to measure the efficacy of their control measures and to quickly rectify any shortcomings.

Some of the studies during the early phase of the pandemic in Saudi Arabia showed very good knowledge of COVID-19 and related issues among the respondents (Al-Hanawi et al., 2020). Although it is quite difficult to make the comparisons between different studies, there are some similar patterns seen regarding the knowledge on COVID-19 and its control measures. As most studies were conducted online during the pandemic, it can be asserted that the respondents would be those highly literate with good access to online communications.

8.2.2 Malaysian previous studies

A study done locally by Azlan et al. (2020) showed that Malaysians have moderate knowledge of the nature and transmission of the COVID-19 infection. However, there was a large variance in the correct scores with lower scores seen among male respondents aged less than 50 and those within the low-income category. Similarly, a high level of knowledge regarding COVID-19 prevention was also observed among the office workers and highly educated Vietnamese respondents (Van Nhu et al., 2020) and the highly educated respondents in Arab Saudi (Mansuri et al., 2020). However, in a lower-income country such as Bangladesh, it was found that a notably low of 33% of their people has good knowledge related to COVID-19 and its preventive measures (Paul et al., 2020). Furthermore, approximately half of the respondents were confused with the importance of wearing a face mask, which was mainly attributed to the government's indecisive response on this matter.

8.2.3 Some important messages from the studies

Some of the important messages were obtained from those studies. It is important to take into account, the different levels of literacy among the public during the dissemination of information. Various mediums of communication need to be utilised such as regular reminders through mobile phones (Van Nhu et al. 2020) and television public service campaigns (Zhong et al., 2020). Information given should also be short and precise and the use of infographics, for example, was more reliable and easy acceptable compared to long texts (Egan et al., 2021). Further, the studies revealed that poor understanding of the pandemic issue prevented effective recovery as knowledge is highly associated with a positive attitude and good practice. Worse, the studies suggested that this could lead to a sense of fear and panic, as well as non-compliance to the control measures (Paul et al., 2020).

Apart from a good knowledge of the COVID-19 situation, the public's positive attitudes and adherence towards the measures taken have largely been attributed to public confidence towards the government's efforts (Azlan et al, 2020; Zhong et al., 2020). The COVID-19 pandemic has been an unprecedented event and has significantly changed the lifestyle and behaviour of the public. Thus, it was not surprising to see a large percentage of people struggle and have difficulty complying with the new norm. Likewise, a positive attitude would be achieved if they were confident with the government's plan and achievable outcomes (Van Nhu et al., 2020). Several global scale studies showed that a solid trust in the government's efforts will create a positive perception among the public which eventually influence their behaviours and adherence to the necessary control measures (Al-Hasan et al., 2020; Lazarus et al., 2020).

8.2.4 Reasons for non-compliances

In addition to the surveys conducted, several other studies sought to investigate the reasons for non-compliance towards the preventive measures which had been implemented. Two different studies were conducted on the public's compliance on social distancing, one among the youth in Switzerland (Nivette et al., 2021) and the other among the general public in the United Kingdom (Hills and Eraso, 2021). While the Switzerland youth highly complied with social distancing but not to hygiene-related measures, the British people were found to intentionally violate social distancing. Interestingly, studies linked the non-compliance practice to an anti-social factor namely having a lower sense of social responsibility. In addition, a study in South Korea found that high violation toward self-quarantine measures were due to fear of losing income despite high penalty imposed (Ryu et al., 2020).

8.2.5 Significance of this study

Our study will provide additional insights into the public's KAP on the health and legal measures that were carried out in Malaysia during the second wave of the pandemic in the country. Understanding the measures, having the appropriate attitudes and good practices would give guidance to the authorities in making sure the measures imposed are complied with and help the people to adapt to the new life normalcy. We have aimed to determine the scores in each component of the KAP and also try to identify relevant factors associated with the KAP scores.

KAP surveys have been used since 1950's especially in the field of health science mainly in public health (Launiala, 2009). Ideally, a KAP survey should precede awareness or an intervention program. The KAP assessment tool aims to obtain what is known (knowledge), thought (attitude), and performed (practiced) in the context of the topic of interest (Andrade et al., 2020). This instrument is used to examine knowledge and behaviour to identify substantial gaps between what is said and what is done (Gumucio et al., 2011) in health crises.

In the current COVID-19 pandemic, many KAP surveys were conducted in the general well as in selected subpopulations, including health care workers (Andrade et al., 2020). Due to novel situation of COVID-19 and the changes of standard regulations and guidelines, determining public behavioural change is crucial in flattening the COVID-19 infection curve. Study on KAP towards measures of preventing the spread of COVID-19 is very essential in determining the knowledge about the disease and society's readiness to comply with the standard regulation and guidelines established by the government. KAP study can be used as preliminary information by the relevant authorities to develop further intervention and proper health promotion in order to mitigate the spread of the disease (Azlan et al., 2020).

8.3 Methodology

8.3.1 Questionnaires

We conducted an online cross-sectional survey among the adult general population in Malaysia from June 2020 until August 2020, during the RMCO period. Questionnaires were designed via Google Form with links to the survey shared through various social media platforms and the contact list. Ethical approval was obtained from the Human Ethics Committee of Universiti Sains Islam Malaysia before distributing the questionnaires.

The questionnaires development involved four researchers, two experts in public health, and two experts in the law and legislation field. The background and study objectives were clearly described on the first page of the online survey. We disseminated the questionnaires in English as well as in the national language Malay to all adults residing in the country. To reach as many respondents as possible, we shared the link to the questionnaires through social media namely *Facebook* and *Whatsapp*.

The questionnaire consisted of 16 questions related to the health and legal measures in Malaysia. The questions were divided into four sections, namely demographic and the respondents' responses in terms of their knowledge, attitude, and practice on the health and legal measures implemented in the country. Respondents stated their knowledge on the measures by choosing yes, no, and do not know. One mark was given for every correct answer and zero marks for incorrect and not sure. Likewise, the five-point Likert scale was used to measure respondents' attitudes and practice in adhering to the government's measures. Subsequently, we calculated the total and mean score for each component.

We also statistically analysed the data for percentage and frequencies. Bivariate analysis was conducted to determine the significant association between the scores with other variables, and the value of $p < 0.05$ was taken as the significant level.

8.3.2 Study limitations

This study has several limitations. As the questionnaires were delivered through online platform, we could not get the responses from various levels of people within the community. Some of them may not have access to the Internet, while others may be illiterate or not using the social media where we had posted the invitation to participate in the study. Although we have conducted a valid sampling method, the respondents were overrepresented from those of educated groups. In addition, this study was performed during the second wave of the pandemic in 2020 and at the early phase of MCO, where the respondents might have been more vigilant at that time than now. Hence, we suggest a repeat survey using the same questionnaire to gauge the differences of responses if there were indications of information fatigue as experienced in other countries.

8.4 Findings and discussion

8.4.1 Characteristics of respondents

A total of 550 respondents answered the survey and were included in the final analysis, of which 72% were female. Almost all respondents were Malaysian (99%). About 92% of the respondents received tertiary education with 53% of the total respondents working as professionals.

Table 8.2 Demographic characteristics of respondents
(Total respondents = 550)

Variables		Number (percentage)
Gender	Male	154 (28%)
	Female	396 (72%)
Citizenship	Malaysian	544 (99%)
	Non-Malaysian	6 (1%)
Education	Secondary	42 (8%)
	College/University	508 (92%)
Occupation	Professional	290 (53%)
	Non-professional	99 (18%)
	Not working/housewife	51 (9%)
	Students	99 (18%)
	Pensioner	11 (2%)
Source of	Official webpage	291 (53%)
information	Social media	263 (48%)
	News	259 (47%)
	Friends/ family/workplace	87 (16%)

The respondents had received their information primarily from the official webpage of the Ministry of Health (53%) followed by the mainstream media (48%), social media namely *Facebook* and *Twitter* (47%), while a small percentage (16%) relied on the information shared by their family, friends, and workmates (16%) (Table 8.2).

8.4.2 Knowledge of health and legal measures

We found that the knowledge scores were high for all the questions asked. The mean score was 7.7 (SD: 0.78) over 8 with approximately 85% of the respondents achieved scored above average (Table 8.3). This indicates that most respondents have good knowledge on the health and legal measures related to COVID-19. As our respondents consisted of largely graduate professionals, the high scores related to their knowledge were expected from this highly literate group. They have better access to the widely available information online and are expected to be proficient in information-seeking skills. It is important to note that the survey was conducted at the early stage of the pandemic where people, in general, were still curious and had self-motivation to seek as much information as possible. A considerable amount of literature published also showed similar high and adequate knowledge towards the government measures as seen in respondents

Table 8.3 Mean scores of knowledge, attitude, and practice
of respondents towards health and legal measures
related to COVID-19 (Total respondents = 550)

Variables	Mean score (standard deviation)	Number of respondents (percentage)	
		High score	Equal/low score
Knowledge (Total score: 8)	7.77 (0.78)	467 (84.9%)	83 (15.1%)
Attitude (Total score: 35)	31.98 (4.60)	373 (67.8%)	177 (32.2%)
Practice (Total score: 20)	16.99 (3.23)	327 (59.5%)	223 (40.5%)

from Switzerland (Selby et al., 2020); Saudi Arabia (Mansuri et al., 2020), and China (Zhang et al., 2020).

The majority of respondents answered correctly on the ways to avoid transmission, which include avoiding the 3C, i.e., crowded places (99% correct), confined spaces (88%), and close conversation (98%) (Figure 8.1). The high scores were likely attributed to the overwhelming coverage of the SOPs in the media. It also indicates the public understanding of the information shared with them on the mode of transmission and the necessary self-precaution that they

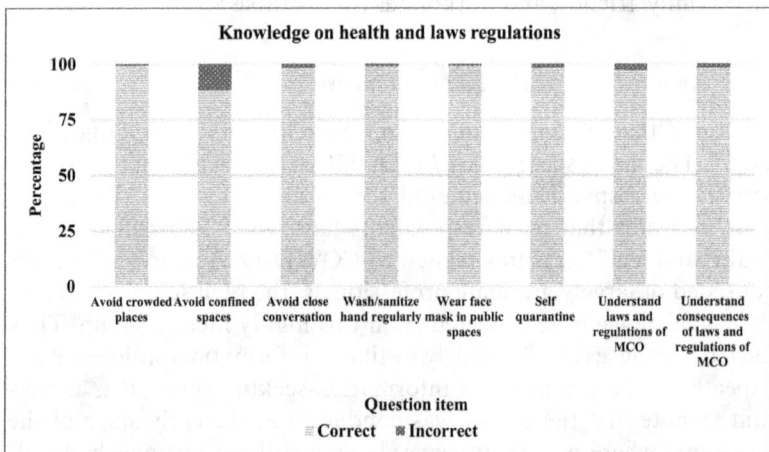

Figure 8.1 The percentage of response on the knowledge questions on health and laws regulations implemented in Malaysia.

can undertake. Furthermore, respondents also understood the value of wearing a face mask, especially in public spaces (99%) and the importance of self-quarantine once in contact with a positive case of COVID-19 (98%). In terms of the legal measures, 97% of the respondents understood the laws and regulations related to the MCO and 98% knew the consequences of disobeying the MCO laws and regulations (Figure 8.1).

The knowledge scores significantly differed between males and females (Table 8.4). Female respondents were found to be more knowledgeable than male respondents (p = 0.010). The findings that females' respondents were more knowledgeable and have better practice than males were expected with similar patterns reported in other populations from Saudi (Al-Hanawi et al., 2020) and Switzerland (Selby et al., 2020). As Selby et al. (2020) had pointed out in their study, females have higher worry level and therefore seek more knowledge to protect themselves. Scores were also higher among respondents with tertiary education and professional workers. Although the differences were not statistically significant, it shows the ability of the educated group to acquired knowledge and has better access to various information portals. It can be assumed that higher educated persons are more likely to observe good health measures, and therefore, more studies are needed to examine knowledge among lower educated groups.

Table 8.4 Factors associated with knowledge of respondents towards health and legal measures related to COVID-19 (Total respondents = 550)

Variables	Number of respondents (percentage)		Statistical difference between categories
	High score	*Low score*	*p-value*
Gender			
Male	121 (78.6)	33 (21.4)	**0.010***
Female	346 (87.4)	50 (12.6)	
Education level			
Secondary	37 (88.1)	5(11.9)	0.548
University/college	430 (84.6)	78 (15.4)	
Occupation			
Professional	250 (86.2)	40 (13.8)	0.106
Non-professional	88 (88.9)	11 (11.1)	
Others	129 (80.1)	32 (19.9)	

Note: *p-value of <0.05 is considered as statistically significant.

8.4.3 Attitude toward health and legal measures

We asked seven questions to assess the respondents' attitudes on obtaining information and obeying the MCOs. The mean score for attitude was 31.9 (SD: 4.6) out of 35, with approximately 68% of the respondents scored marks above average (Table 8.3). Majority of the respondents (93%) agreed that it is essential to get the reliable and latest information on MCO. This may indicate their concern on the situation and crisis, and therefore, it is suggested that the authorities continue to disseminate information that is essential for health concerned communities (Table 8.5).

With the various SOPs implemented during the MCOs, most of the respondents agreed to obey the related laws and regulations (94%), and mainly their agreement was to avoid punishment (93%). Likewise, 95% will obey SOPs when going out (Table 8.5). Although the best scenario will be inculcating the public's self-conscience and responsibility, the authorities will always need to draw a clear line between what is legal and what is not to avoid confusion.

Interestingly, the respondents also felt that the need to ensure that their family members follow suit (95%) and could not tolerate other

Table 8.5 Attitude of respondents towards health and legal measures related to COVID-19 (N = 550)

Attitude	Negative response N (percentage)	Neutral response N (percentage)	Positive response N (percentage)
• I get reliable information about the MCO	10 (1.9%)	24 (4.4%)	516 (93.9%)
• I get latest information about the MCO	10 (1.9%)	28 (5.1%)	512 (93.1%)
• I obey the laws and regulations of MCO	14 (2.1%)	17 (3.15%)	519 (94.4%)
• I obey the laws and regulations to avoid punishment	14 (2.9%)	22 (4.0%)	512 (93.1%)
• I follow the SOPs when going out	12 (2.1%)	11 (2.0%)	427 (95.8%)
• I always ensure my family obey the laws and regulations of MCO	10 (1.8%)	19 (3.5%)	521 (94.7%)
• I could not tolerate society who disobeyed the MCO regulations	18 (3.3%)	33 (6.0%)	499 (90.7%)

Table 8.6 Factors associated with attitude of respondents towards health and legal measures related to COVID-19 (Total respondents = 550)

Variables	Number of respondents (percentage)		Statistical difference between categories
	High score	Low score	p-value
Gender			
Male	97(63.0)	57(37.0)	0.130
Female	276(69.7)	120(30.3)	
Education level			
Secondary	27(64.3)	15(35.7)	0.610
University/college	346(68.1)	162(31.9)	
Occupation			
Professional	208(71.7)	82(28.3)	0.098
Non-professional	65(65.7)	34 (34.3)	
Others	100(62.1)	61(37.9)	

Note: p-value of <0.05 is considered as statistically significant.

people who disobeyed the MCO regulations (90%). These positive attitudes showed the respondents' willingness to unite and take care of each other during the challenging period. There were no significant association of the sociodemographic characteristics with the attitude (Table 8.6). Nevertheless, we found out a significant relationship between having a good attitude with good practice among the respondents (p < 0.001) (Table 8.8). Apart from self-understanding of the situation and the consequences, as seen in the good knowledge score, the positive attitude was most likely influenced by the government's strict measures, including fines and/or imprisonment against violators (Yeoh and Qarirah, 2020).

8.4.4 Practice related to health and legal measures

Regarding the practice taken, the mean score for practice was 16.9 (SD: 3.2) out of 20 with more than half (59%) scored above average (Table 8.3). Approximately 93% of the respondents follow regular updates from the Ministry of Health (Table 8.7). This most likely happened during the early stage of the pandemic where daily updates on the situation were given by the Director General of Health and broadcast-to all media channels. Similarly, SMSs were regularly sent by the National Security Council to the whole nation. This suggests the value

Table 8.7 Practices of respondents towards health and legal
measures related to COVID-19 (N = 550)

Practice	Negative response N (percentage)	Neutral response N (percentage)	Positive response N (percentage)
I follow regular updates on COVID-19 information by the Ministry of Health	13 (2.0%)	29 (5.3%)	510 (92.7%)
I educate other people near me to obey the rules and regulations	31 (5.7%)	78 (14.2%)	441 (80.2%)
I warn people who disobey the rules and regulations during MCO	55 (10.0%)	111 (20.2%)	384 (69.8%)

Table 8.8 Factors associated with practices of respondents
towards health and legal measures related to
COVID-19 (Total respondents = 550)

Variables	Number of respondents (percentage)		Statistical difference between categories
	High score	Low score	p-value
Gender			
Male	79(51.3)	75(48.7)	**0.015***
Female	248(62.6)	148(37.4)	
Education level			
Secondary	25(59.5)	17(40.5)	0.992
University/college	302(59.4)	206(40.6)	
Occupation			
Professional	182(62.8)	108(37.2)	0.249
Non-professional	55(55.6)	44(44.4)	
Others	90(55.9)	71(44.1)	
Knowledge			
Poor	42(50.6)	41(49.4)	0.075
Good	285(61.0)	182(39.0)	
Attitude			
Poor	52(29.4)	125(70.6)	**<0.001***
Good	275(73.7)	98(26.3)	

Note: *p-value of <0.05 is considered as statistically significant.

of a reliable source of information that needs to be continued in the long term.

A lesser percentage (80%) took the effort to educate other people, and about 69% will warn other people who disobey MCO's rules and regulations. Compared with the good attitude when it involves other people, there was a relatively lesser percentage of respondents practising them, most probably related to their level of assertiveness. The public should be encouraged to help in promoting good behaviour and practices within the community to mitigate the impact of COVID-19. Like the knowledge, we also found that female respondents significantly have better scores than males ($p = 0.015$) (Table 8.8).

8.5 Conclusion

8.5.1 Communication of health and legal measures

This study's findings revealed important information regarding Malaysian people's KAP of the government's measures during the COVID-19 pandemic. The results were also timely to the government's and health authority's proactive and well-coordinated management. Our findings indicated that the general population relies on information and statements from the official sources, i.e., the Ministry of Health Malaysia and had good knowledge, attitude, and practice regarding the health and legal measures implemented. The respondents' good understanding and positive attitudes have been reflected in their adherence and practice towards the government's measures. People who understand the situation can generally open up and accept any changes, even if it is far from their regular practice.

While the MCO is rather strict, the SOPs often change depending on the current situation and risk assessment done by the Ministry of Health. Any changes are often found through the regularly updated official websites and usually shared through messaging apps, namely *WhatsApp* and *Telegram*. Although some changes may be inevitable, they need to be notified early to the public to minimise the disruption to their everyday life and at the same time to minimise the anxiety level. We, therefore, suggest that excellent understanding could only be made possible if the government and the authorities practice effective communication and lead by example. In times of uncertainty, many people rely on a source and a figure that they could trust and put their hopes. Every word or action from a credible leader not only promotes cooperation from the public but at the same time building trust and emotional support. Consistency and transparency are the keys to success in implementing health and legal measures regardless of one's status.

8.5.2 Ensuring compliance

Many other countries, in Europe, are also compelled to issue punishment, particularly when civil obedience began to lax with time (Bisserbe et al., 2020). Some experts believe that during public health emergencies as in the COVID-19 pandemic, strict fines and punishments may be introduced and necessary, particularly when everyone is racing against time to protect the country's economic and healthcare system. However, these measures may not be sustainable in the long term as there will always be a group of non-compliance (Nivette et al., 2021) and the set of pandemic fatigue (WHO, 2020a) that forms a threat towards the public health measures.

8.5.3 Suggestions and recommendations

At the time of this writing, Malaysia is battling with third wave of COVID-19 infection which appears to be more damaging than before. The public needs to be continually educated, and in a multi-cultural and multi-ethnic country like Malaysia, any education and awareness campaign should be able to reach all community levels, particularly those with poor access to the Internet and social media. Guidelines and measures should be realistic and achievable. The government needs to listen to people's needs and concerns during this challenging time and support any shortcomings. Furthermore, trust in the authorities needs to be sustained as this will influence their attitude and practice in many aspects of mitigation measures. However, as we reached the one-year pandemic anniversary, some people tend to be complacent with the measures and restrictions despite consistent reminders and education. Consequently, starting March 2021, the government had increased the maximum amount of compound to RM10,000 for a repeat violation of the MCO SOP (The Sun Daily, 2021).

8.5.4 Recommendation for future research

Based on the current situation, a long-term plan needs to be in line. Future studies should aim to include respondents of various socio-economic backgrounds to determine their level of understanding. The recent spike in the number of cases nowadays also requires the survey to be repeated at different phases. However, further face-to-face surveys could be challenging as infodemic tends to grow with time, causing fear and distrust. At the same time, both pandemic and survey fatigue kick in, hence threatening the response rate.

While there are escalating non-compliance cases during the MCO, the spike in daily COVID-19 cases is not solely attributed to, or correlated to, KAP. Other measures introduced are linked to the spike, such as active detection at hotspots (The Star, 2020). Further study also may be required in terms of possible factors leading to KAP, such as risk perception and health literacy (Azlan et al., 2020).

Post-COVID realities and possibilities

The Malaysian government has imposed various health and legal measures to mitigate the impact of COVID-19 infection. Our study revealed that most Malaysian respondents had good knowledge and favourable attitude and practised towards the health and legal measures implemented in the country, particularly at the early stage of the pandemic. The impact of knowledge was enormous as it allows understanding of the situation and changes that took place and encouraged people to be resilient during this pandemic crisis. More importantly, knowledge influences people's behaviour and attitude, contributing to their adherence to any mitigating measures imposed. As time goes by, new and sometimes unpredictable challenges emerged. Therefore, it is essential to have well planned, efficient and consistent communication by the government and health authorities to tackle the COVID-19 pandemic.

Acknowledgement

This research was supported by COVID-19 research grant by Universiti Sains Islam Malaysia 2020 PPPI/COVID19_0120/FPSK/051000/16320. We would like to thank the university and the reviewers on the grant and comments.

References

Al-Hanawi, M. K., Angawi, K., Alshareef, N., Qattan, A., Helmy, H. Z., Abudawood, Y., Alqurashi, M., Kattan, W. M., Kadasah, N. A., Chirwa, G. C., & Alsharqi, O. (2020). Knowledge, attitude and practice toward COVID-19 among the public in the Kingdom of Saudi Arabia: A cross-sectional study. *Frontiers in Public Health*, 8, 217. Retrieved from https://doi.org/10.3389/fpubh.2020.00217.

Al-Hasan, A., Yim, D., & Khuntia, J. (2020). Citizens' adherence to COVID-19 mitigation recommendations by the government: A 3-country comparative evaluation using web-based cross-sectional survey data. *Journal of Medical Internet Research*, 22(8), e20634. Retrieved from https://doi.org/10.2196/20634.

Andrade, C., Menon, V., Ameen, S., & Kumar Praharaj, S. (2020). Designing and conducting knowledge, attitude, and practice surveys in psychiatry: Practical guidance. *Indian Journal of Psychological Medicine*, 42(5), 478–481.

Aziz, N. A., Othman, J., Lugova, H., & Suleiman, A. (2020). Malaysia's approach in handling COVID-19 onslaught: Report on the Movement Control Order (MCO) and targeted screening to reduce community infection rate and impact on public health and economy. *Journal of Infection and Public Health*, 13(12), 1823–1829. Retrieved from https://doi.org/10.1016/j.jiph.2020.08.007.

Azlan, A. A., Hamzah, M. R., Sern, T. J., Ayub, S. H., & Mohamad, E. (2020). Public knowledge, attitudes and practices towards COVID-19: A cross-sectional study in Malaysia. *PLOS One*, 15(5), e0233668. Retrieved from https://doi.org/10.1371/journal.pone.0233668.

Bisserbe, N., Sylvers, E., & Martinez, M. (2020, October 19). As COVID-19 roars back in europe, governments get tougher on rule breakers. WSJ website. Retrieved from https://www.wsj.com/articles/as-COVID-19-roars-back-in-europe-governments-get-tougher-on-rule-breakers-11603111859.

Carlos, W. G., Cruz, C. S. D., CAo, B., Pasnick, S., & Jamil, S. (2020). Novel Wuhan (2019-nCoV) coronavirus. *American Journal of Respiratory and Critical Care Medicine*, 201(4), 7–8. Retrieved from https://doi.org/10.1164/rccm.2014P7.

Claeson, M. & Hanson, S. (2021). COVID-19 and the Swedish enigma. *The Lancet*, 397(10271), 259–261. Retrieved from https://doi.org/10.1016/S0140-6736(20)32750-1.

Egan, M., Acharya, A., Sounderajah, V., Xu, Y., Mottershar, A. et al. (2021). Evaluating the effect of infographics on public recall, sentiment and willingness to use face masks during the COVID-19 pandemic: A randomised internet-based questionnaire study. *BMC Public Health*, 21, 367. Retrieved from https://doi.org/10.1186/s12889-021-10356-0.

Gumucio, S., Merica, M., Luhmann, N., Fauvel, G., Zompi, S., Ronsse, A., Fauvel, G., Courcaud, A., Bouchon M., Trehin, C., Schapman, S., & Ronsse, R. (2011). Data collection quantitative methods, the KAP survey model (Knowledge, Attitude and Practices). *IGC communigraphie; Saint Etienne, France, 5.*

Hills, S. & Eraso, Y. (2021). Factors associated with non-adherence to social distancing rules during the COVID-19 pandemic: A logistic regression analysis. *BMC Public Health* 21, 352. Retrieved from https://doi.org/10.1186/s12889-021-10379-7.

Kalil, A. C. (2020). Treating COVID-19—Off-label drug use, compassionate use, and randomised clinical trials during pandemics. *JAMA*, 323(19), 1897–1898. Retrieved from https://doi.org/10.1001/jama.2020.4742.

Launiala, A. (2009). How much can a KAP survey tell us about people's knowledge, attitudes and practices? Some observations from medical anthropology research on malaria in pregnancy in Malawi. *Anthropology Matters*, 11(1), 1–13. Retrieved from https://doi.org/10.22582/am.v11i1.31

Lazarus, J. V., Ratzan, S., Palayew, A., Billari, F. C., Binagwaho, A., et al. (2020). COVID-SCORE: A global survey to assess public perceptions of government responses to COVID-19 (COVID-SCORE-10). *PLOS One*, 15(10), e0240011. Retrieved from https://doi.org/10.1371/journal.pone.0240011.

Mansuri, F. M. A., Zalat, M. M., Khan, A. A., Alsaedi, E. Q., & Ibrahim, H. M. (2020). Estimating the public response to mitigation measures and self-perceived behaviours towards the COVID-19 pandemic. *Journal of Taibah University Medical Sciences*, 15(4), 278–283. Retrieved from https://doi.org/10.1016/j.jtumed.2020.06.003.

National Security Council Act 2016 (Act 776). Retrieved from http://www.federalgazette.agc.gov.my/outputaktap/aktaBI_20160607_776-BI.pdf.

Nivette, A., Ribeaud, D., Murray, A., Steinhoff, A., Bechtiger, L., Hepp, U., Shanahan, L., & Eisner, M. (2021). Non-compliance with COVID-19-related public health measures among young adults in Switzerland: Insights from a longitudinal cohort study. *Social Science & Medicine*, 268, 113370. Retrieved from https://doi.org/10.1016/j.socscimed.2020.113370.

Paul, A., Sikdar, D., Hossain, M. M., Amin, M. R., Deeba, F. et al. (2020). Knowledge, attitudes, and practices toward the novel coronavirus among Bangladeshis: Implications for mitigation measures. *PLOS One*, 15(9), e0238492. Retrieved from https://doi.org/10.1371/journal.pone.0238492.

Police Act 1967 (Act 344). Retrieved from http://www.agc.gov.my/Akta/Vol.%207/Act%20344.pdf.

Prevention and Control of Infectious Disease (Measures within the infected local areas) regulations 2020. Published 18 March 2020. Retrieved from http://www.federalgazette.agc.gov.my/outputp/pua_20200318_PUA91_2020.pdf.

Ryu, S., Hwang, Y., Yoon, H., & Chun, B. (2020). Self-quarantine noncompliance during the COVID-19 pandemic in South Korea. *Disaster Medicine and Public Health Preparedness*, 1–4. Retrieved from https://doi:10.1017/dmp.2020.374.

Selby, K., Durand, M.-A., Gouveia, A., Bosisio, F., Barazzetti, G., Hostettler, M., D'Acremont, V., Kaufmann, A., & von Plessen, C. (2020). Citizen responses to government restrictions in switzerland during the COVID-19 pandemic: Cross-sectional survey. *JMIR Formative Research*, 4(12), e20871. Retrieved from https://doi.org/10.2196/20871.

Tang, K.H.D. (2020). Movement control as an effective measure against COVID-19 spread in Malaysia: an overview. *Zeitschrift fur Gesundheitswissenschaften = Journal of public health*, 1–4. Advance online publication. Retrieved from https://doi.org/10.1007/s10389-020-01316-w.

Teoh, P.Y. & Basyir M. (2021) COVID-19 vaccine not an 'immunity passsport', New Straits Time, 4th January (Online). Retrieved from https://www.nst.com.my/news/nation/2021/01/654482/COVID-19-vaccine-not-immunity-passport;accessed. (Accessed: 10 January 2021).

The Lancet. (2020). COVID-19: fighting panic with information. *Lancet (London, England)*, 395(10224), 537. Retrieved from https://doi.org/10.1016/s0140-6736(20)30379-2.

The Star (2020). Health DG: Spike in COVID-19 cases expected due to active detection at hotspots. Retrieved from https://www.thestartv.com/v/health-dg-spike-in-covid-19-cases-expected-due-to-active-detection-at-hotspots.

The Sun Daily (2021). Compound for violating MCO SOP now set at RM10,000–IGP. Retrieved from https://www.thesundaily.my/local/compound-for-violating-mco-sop-now-set-at-rm10000-igp-updated-YB7175562.

Turan, B., Budhwani, H., Fazeli, P. L., Browning, W. R., Raper, J. L., Mugavero, M. J., & Turan, J. M. (2016). How does stigma affect people living with HIV? The mediating roles of internalized and anticipated HIV stigma in the effects of perceived community stigma on health and psychosocial outcomes. *AIDS and Behavior*, 21(1), 283–291. Retrieved from https://doi.org/10.1007/s10461-016-1451-5.

Van Nhu, H., Tuyet-Hanh, T. T., Van, N., Linh, T., & Tien, T. Q. (2020). Knowledge, attitudes, and practices of the Vietnamese as key factors in controlling COVID-19. *Journal of community health*, 45(6), 1263–1269. Retrieved from https://doi.org/10.1007/s10900-020-00919-4.

World Health Organization (WHO) (2020a, October 7). WHO/Europe discusses how to deal with pandemic fatigue. Retrieved from https://www.who.int/news-room/feature-stories/detail/who-europe-discusses-how-to-deal-with-pandemic-fatigue.

World Health Organization (WHO). (2020b). Managing the COVID-19 infodemic: Promoting healthy behaviours and mitigating the harm from misinformation and disinformation. Retrieved from https://www.who.int/news/item/23-09-2020-managing-the-COVID-19-infodemic-promoting-healthy-behaviours-and-mitigating-the-harm-from-misinformation-and-disinformation.

World Health Organization (WHO). (2020c). Novel Coronavirus (2019-nCoV): Situation Report - 1. Retrieved from https://www.who.int/docs/default-source/coronaviruse/situation-reports/20200121-sitrep-1-2019-ncov.pdf?sfvrsn=20a99c10_4.

Yeoh, L. & Qarirah, N. (2020, September 14). COVID-19 pandemic and the rule of law. Malaysiakini website. Retrieved from https://www.malaysiakini.com/letters/542531.

Zhang, L., Tao, Y., Shen, M., Fairley, C. K., & Guo, Y. (2020). Can self-imposed prevention measures mitigate the COVID-19 epidemic? *PLOS Medicine*, 17(7), e1003240. Retrieved from https://doi.org/10.1371/journal.pmed.1003240.

Zhong, B. L., Luo, W., Li, H. M., Zhang, Q. Q., Liu, X. G., Li, W. T., & Li, Y. (2020). Knowledge, attitudes, and practices towards COVID-19 among Chinese residents during the rapid rise period of the COVID-19 outbreak: A quick online cross-sectional survey. *International Journal of Biological Sciences*, 16(10), 1745–1752. Retrieved from https://doi.org/10.7150/ijbs.45221.

For Product Safety Concerns and Information please contact our EU
representative GPSR@taylorandfrancis.com
Taylor & Francis Verlag GmbH, Kaufingerstraße 24, 80331 München, Germany

www.ingramcontent.com/pod-product-compliance
Lightning Source LLC
Chambersburg PA
CBHW061743270326
41928CB00011B/2354

* 9 7 8 1 0 3 2 0 2 2 8 7 1 *